Denver MEN in the Kitchen

Enjoy!
Candis
Kloverstrom

Denver MEN in the Kitchen

**Delicious, hot and saucy dishes
from some of
Colorado's most interesting men**

All recipes have been pre-tested.

Candis Kloverstrom

Illustrated & Designed by Candis Kloverstrom
Photography by Candis Kloverstrom
Edited by Barbara Munson

Artistic Impact Publishing, LLC
303-688-0649

PO Box 891
Franktown, CO 80116

Books may be purchased
by contacting the publisher,

Artistic Impact Publishing, LLC

PO Box 891, Franktown, CO 80116

303-688-0649 • fax 303-688-9543

www.DenverMenInTheKitchen.com

Library of Congress Catalog Card #2004090307
ISBN: 0-9721335-1-8
1. cookbook 2. community resource guide
First edition
Printed in Korea

preface—good food, good guys...

Denver Men in the Kitchen is about some of the most successful and interesting men in Denver who happen to like to cook. It's also a celebration of these men. They deserve it.

When I first set out to do this book, I was aware that guys in general didn't seem to be getting enough acknowledgement and praise for the things they did. We women were taking on new roles, new challenging careers and new life styles...and we were getting plenty of recognition. But our "breadwinners" had new roles, too. They were still bringing home the bacon, but more and more of them were also coming home to cook the bacon.

So, I decided to put together a composite picture of some of the guys who are using their talents both at work and at home. Their homes are where they have taken on one of the most challenging roles there is: creating and sharing dishes, i.e., providing for others, delighting others, sharing of themselves. To me, this is a huge undertaking and a leap for many men.

This book is also about why the men do what they do, which is cook. The reasons they cook, I found, are endless! They range from needing to "escape" and relax, to wanting to perfect their grill-meister skills, to serving as the sole family chef, to being a single parent, to occasionally dabbling in the kitchen just because it's fun. And they all are proud of their dishes, no matter the motivation.

I decided I would personally interview each man selected for the book. That's 57 of them! I would meet them outside of their work environments, go beyond the business suits and the titles—to look into their lives and create a more accurate picture of today's successful guy. For the most part, we met in their kitchens and sometimes in mine. I got great recipes and photographs—and the education of a lifetime. I was truly impressed!

The word success keeps cropping up. Sure, there's success at work, but how about success in keeping the home fires burning? Traditionally, we have thought of the male as being the conqueror, the one who provides, and the one who is out on the front line sometimes battling to keep food on the table. I believe there has not been enough emphasis on the importance of the man in the home and the part he plays in keeping all intact. Truth be known, the men who expend effort on building home fires are the ones who also find home fires the warmest.

Looking at what I found over this past year as I developed this book, I saw some other themes: creativity, caring for others, and most importantly, making wise choices. Small, everyday choices that create who we are...choices that influence future events and leave a legacy for future generations. Our families, our health and our happiness are impacted by those choices.

Congratulations all!
Candis Kloverstrom

foreword

Can you believe it? Men in the kitchen—and not just men in the kitchen making a mess, but men in the kitchen actually cooking! That's what *Denver Men in the Kitchen* is all about. It's about the unique blend of culinary preferences and the diverse and eclectic personalities of these fascinating men in Denver. They all, in their own way, have provided a "flavor" that represents them and their personality. Here you'll find a snapshot, or should I say a "slice," of the exquisite flavor of their personal favorites and you'll discover the engaging individuals who make up the fabulous aroma and tastes of Denver.

Just like the special and unique recipes they have contributed, each of these men is special and successful as well. Success is built into every human being. God already created the right blend of ingredients for each of us to live a purposeful, meaningful and successful life. All we have to do is mix and activate those ingredients.

Success is like a box of cake mix. On the outside is a photograph of a picture-perfect cake, but on the inside is simply flour. It doesn't become a cake until you add oil, eggs and water. In fact, on the box it tells you that you must "preheat, grease, flour lightly, blend, beat, pour, bake, and cool." Success in life is the same way. It comes from mixing the right ingredients and taking the right steps.

Every recipe that you find in this book has a list of ingredients and instructions on how to put it all together in the right way with the right steps to create the masterpiece. It reminds me of our own lives. To create a picture-perfect life, we need to add lots of things along the way—laughter, love of others, purpose for life, integrity, character and worthwhile goals. It's only when we mix the right ingredients in our life and add some heat that we come out looking picture perfect.

Someone once said, "A tea bag isn't worth much until it's been through some hot water." It's the heat of the oven that turns the flour, eggs, water and oil into a cake and it's the heat of life that turns all of our "ingredients" into something that's picture perfect.

I believe God has already deposited all the ingredients you need to discover the finished product for life. All you have to do is activate those ingredients.

—*Michael Ware, Senior Pastor, Victory Church*

Salesman extraordinaire, as one of Agilent Technology's top salesmen, Mark Kloverstrom comes complete with an Electrical Engineering degree from the University of Colorado and an MBA from Regis University. As one who has always valued family, he can be counted on to spend time off with wife, children and grandchild. His dedication to a life style of commitment to serving others is evident in the atmosphere and well-being in the Kloverstrom home.

No, this gentleman does not cook. So, why is he in this book? If it were not for his support, this book would never have been possible. It takes more than an idea to bring a heartfelt plan into existence. Mark may not cook, but he does all the dishes! Besides, he is an excellent model, with the very look needed to make the front cover complete. As a fun book, who else but the husband of the author for this very purpose?

All kidding aside, how did he end up on the front cover? When a photo was needed to begin the project, he happened to be in the studio and was snagged for the project. (How many men can say they end up doing things they would never dream if it were not for an aggressive wife?) So, as the project moved forward, a model's photo was planned to replace his photo, but the longer Mark's photo remained on the initial cover design, the more it seemed to fit the look needed. So, he stayed and there you have it!

ﻯ *Mark **Kloverstrom*** ﻯ

dedication & acknowledgements

Many people never express their true calling in life. Because of the relationship I have had with God, my true calling has been realized in this work. And, because of that relationship, I dedicate this book to the God I serve.

A project like this takes many hands to form what is seen within these pages. First and foremost, Barbara Munson, my copy editor, has been instrumental in creating a first-class book. Because she is proficient in her trade, the content and copy editing are excellent. She makes copy sizzle. Thank you, Barbara.

To my attorney, Jon Tandler, who was invaluable for his assistance in developing the legal entities that I needed. And to Katherine Carol, my business coach—her counsel was instrumental in getting me where I am today with my business. As a business coach, she is top-notch.

Thank you to Cecelia Mesa and Suzanne Arguello for taking time to assist with the final editing.

Colorado Independent Publishers Association is an organization I have been hanging around the past couple of years. It consists of a group of savvy self-publishing authors and its motto is, "Do it yourself...without doing it alone." A big thank you, CIPA, for your encouragement, advice and counsel. I would not even be doing books today if I had not first hung around a few self-publishing authors. Thank you.

Mike Jenson with Jenson Advertising gave his time when he was already pushed to the limit with his other projects. Thank you, Mike, for going beyond the call of duty in assisting me with the color corrections and the final review of the layout.

To the many people who helped test all the recipes, thank you. This includes Tony's Meats for supplying at cost some of the ingredients for testing and also for providing some of the photographs I used. And Eric Kloverstrom, my son, spent many hours in my kitchen testing recipes. Thank you.

Pastor Michael Ware, thank you for the Foreword. You have put into words my heart. Thank you for the hours you spent in preparing just the right message for this book.

To my husband, I give a big round of thanks and acknowledgement. He was there behind the scenes, encouraging, counseling, picking up the pieces where needed, even doing my wash for a month so I could get this book out.

—Candis Kloverstrom

hot fish & saucy seafood

boiled shrimp • redfish on the half shell • shrimp with arugula • baja fish tacos with tropical salsa • grouper with capers • marinated tequila, jalapeño shrimp • shrimp creole • filé gumbo • oven baked salmon • red snapper vera cruz • tony's peppered shrimp • citrus salmon • easy cajun catfish • shrimp with lemon-garlic butter • simple salmon • citrus grilled halibut • linguini with clams • stir-fried scallops with asparagus • stuffed lake trout • tortilla-crusted shrimp with fettuccine in corn and poblano cream sauce

not-screwed-up boiled shrimp

William (Bill) H. Stuart, KCNC Channel 4 News

Bill's pet gripe: "Ever eat mushy boiled shrimp? Bad, huh? They were cooked too long. Here's how to make perfect shrimp."

1 bottle of zatarain crab & shrimp boil spice

several lemons

3-4 pounds shrimp, approximately

ice

In a large pot, bring shrimp boil spice and lemons to a boil. Bill says, "I usually use a brand named Zatarain in powder form and several lemons."

Squeeze the juice from the lemons into the water and also toss in the lemon halves. Once the water is boiling fast, dump in the shrimp all at once.

The shrimp are best if just caught but you can use previously frozen shrimp, defrosted. The shrimp must still be in their shells.

As soon as the water returns to a boil pour the shrimp into a colander and cover with ice to stop the cooking process. Timing is critical to avoid overcooked shrimp.

During the summers when he was growing up, Bill worked on shrimp boats and had a job stacking dynamite.

Ӱ *Bill Stuart* Ӱ

Bill Stuart, Anchor Man

KCNC-TV Channel 4 News

Most people recognize Bill Stuart from KCNC-TV, Channel 4, and know him by his reassuring smile and presence. Could it be that Southern charm? Bill grew up in Pascagoula, Mississippi, living by a beach where fishing was a life style and primary food source.

"I'm from a big family of cooks," Bill says, "and it just came naturally."When it comes to fish, his repertoire covers everything from shrimp to grouper to redfish. He also likes to make up new recipes.

So, how did Bill Stuart become an anchorman at a Denver television station? One thing often leads to another to another; so with Bill Stuart. As a high school senior, he worked as a disc jockey for WACY radio. Then he continued on to college at the University of Southern Mississippi. From there he joined the Army where he worked as an Army newspaperman in Hawaii. That path eventually led Bill to Denver.

redfish on the half shell

William (Bill) H. Stuart, KCNC Channel 4 News

As a Louisiana born and bred Southern gentleman, Bill Stuart knows first-hand the ins and outs of catching and cooking good fish.

This is for adventurous cooks! First, catch a redfish. Bill recommends one from Louisiana. Fillet the fish, leaving the skin and scales on. Season the fleshy side generously with garlic, oregano and your favorite spicy seafood seasoning, such as Old Bay or Emeril's Essence. Drizzle with melted butter.

Cook fillet skin-side down on a hot grill with the lid closed until the flesh flakes and separates from the skin. The cooked fillet can be eaten directly from the now-hardened "half shell." Serve with lemon or lime wedges.

shrimp with arugula

William (Bill) H. Stuart, KCNC Channel 4 News

Shrimp is also in Bill's extensive repertoire.

1 pound raw shrimp, peeled

olive oil

butter

2 cloves garlic, minced or chopped

1 small onion, chopped

1 roasted red pepper

1/2 cup dry white wine

1-2 tablespoons flour

arugula

orzo

Sauté shrimp in equal parts olive oil and butter until the shrimp turns pink. Remove from skillet and set aside. Add garlic and onion to skillet and cook until soft. Add about half of the roasted red pepper and let cook for a couple of minutes. Add about one-half cup of dry white wine. You may need to thicken this mixture slightly with a small amount of flour. Add the shrimp back in and heat until warmed.

Just before serving add a large handful of arugula and cook just until the arugula is wilted. Serve over orzo.

baja fish tacos with tropical salsa

Michael (Mick) Rosacci, Tony's Meats & Specialty Foods

Serves four. Mick's recipes are all to-die-for.

fruit salsa (see recipe below)

baja spice rub (see recipe below)

1-1/2 pounds firm-fleshed, boneless fish

2 limes cut into wedges

1 package tortillas, corn or flour

shredded cabbage or lettuce

1 can black beans

Prepare salsa and let the mixture rest for at least one hour so flavors can marry; taste and adjust.

Pre-heat the grill, grilling pan or broiler. Combine spice rub ingredients and sprinkle over the fish. Grill quickly over a very hot, oiled grill to brown and sear on both sides—take care not to overcook! Remove from the grill and drizzle with squeezed lime.

Serve taco style with tortillas, lettuce and beans. This works well with mahi mahi, sea bass, swordfish, tuna, snapper, catfish or shrimp.

Fruit Salsa: Combine half of a large onion, minced; one large tomato, chopped; one ripe mango or papaya, chopped; three-to-four tablespoons minced cilantro; one or two jalapeños, minced; juice of one lime; two tablespoons olive oil; one teaspoon sea salt; one-half teaspoon sugar; one-half teaspoon pepper.

Baja Spice Rub: Combine one teaspoon fine sea salt; one-fourth teaspoon each of dried oregano, cumin, granulated garlic, granulated onion, pepper and chili powder; one-half teaspoon sugar; one-eighth teaspoon cayenne.

grouper with capers

William (Bill) H. Stuart, KCNC Channel 4 News

As a Southern gentleman, this man is an expert on how to make good fish.

Salt, pepper and lightly flour grouper fillet. Brown slowly in skillet with equal parts olive oil and butter. Remove fillet to warm plate. Add capers, white wine, lemon juice and fresh herbs of your choice (such as parsley, oregano, thyme, tarragon) to skillet and briefly cook. Add enough cream to make a nice sauce. Return the fish fillets to pan and continue cooking until the fish flakes. Do not overcook the fish. Serve over pasta.

Rob Reuteman, Business Editor

Rocky Mountain News

If he's not at his desk at the Rocky Mountain News, Rob Reuteman might be out skiing, playing city league softball or training for a 10K race. But you never know. Being business editor at the newspaper also keeps him out and about. "When you get around town," he points out, "you get to know people who eventually become your friends."

As with other Denver Men in the Kitchen, attending college—away from Mom's cooking—was the impetus to start his culinary pursuits. Today, Rob does a lot of barbecuing on weekends where he sizzles up his specialties to enjoy throughout the week.

In 1973, Rob was building homes in Boulder. After receiving a Masters in Journalism in 1978 at the University of Colorado at Boulder, he began working for the daily paper in Golden and then in Longmont. At the Rocky Mountain News he has been an editor since 1983, business editor since 1997.

marinated tequila, jalapeño shrimp

Robert Reuteman, Rocky Mountain News

Rob likes to barbecue this dish on weekends and then enjoy leftovers after a long day at work. This recipe is also excellent for entertaining.

1/3 cup tequila

2 tablespoons canola oil

2 tablespoons fresh lime juice

1 tablespoon minced garlic

2 diced jalapeños

1/2 teaspoon ground red chipotle

1/2 teaspoon powdered sage

1/2 teaspoon white pepper

6 very large shrimp

1 each red and green pepper

5-7 scallions

5 or more romano tomatoes

Mix first eight ingredients; place the shrimp in a large zip-lock bag; pour the marinade mixture over the shrimp. Marinate for about four hours.

Thread the shrimp alternately with the peppers, onions, and tomatoes on a skewer. You can add or substitute any other of your favorite veggies.

Barbecue over low-to-medium heat for about three-to-five minutes on each side until the shrimp is done. The veggies should be slightly crunchy.

Jerry McKissack, President

McKissack Printing & Graphics, Inc.

Jerry McKissack is a third generation Coloradoan and comes from a long line of cooks. He recalls how, as a young child, he would scoot a chair up to the kitchen stove while his father prepared his delectable delights. Taking it all in, Jerry got his first experience on how food contributes to a healthy, loving family environment. He especially remembers his Dad flipping pancakes and preparing biscuits and gravy Sunday mornings.

Today, Jerry does most of the cooking for his household; in fact his children prefer his cooking. As a legacy from his father, his recipes have never been written down, but rather they have been passed to him and on to his son. This book is his chance to finally preserve these delicacies for posterity.

Looking for a printer? McKissack Printing and Graphics has been in business since 1985 and Jerry has been named "Master Craftsman" in color work by the Master Printers of America Association.

shrimp creole

Jerry N. McKissack, McKissack Printing & Graphics, Inc.

This dish is mouth-watering but make sure you reduce the liquid to one inch.

1 stick butter

1-1/2 cups chopped white onion

1 cup chopped celery

1 medium green and 1 medium red bell pepper, diced

2 bay leaves, crushed

5 cloves fresh garlic, minced

1 tablespoon chopped parsley

1 teaspoon each salt and pepper

1/4 teaspoon cayenne pepper

1 cup water

1 fifteen-ounce can tomato sauce

2 pounds medium peeled shrimp

6 cups steamed rice

In a large, deep skillet, melt butter over medium heat and sauté onion, celery, diced bell peppers, garlic and bay leaves until tender.

Stir in tomato sauce, water and all other seasonings; simmer uncovered for ten minutes.

Add the shrimp; cover pan and simmer on low heat for another thirty minutes. Check to see if more water is needed; you should have approximately one inch of liquid in bottom of pan when finished. Serve over steamed rice.

Jerry McKissack

Michael Ware, Senior Pastor

Victory Church

Pastor Mike was once a corporate executive who moved with the movers and shakers; he knew how to run a business and was successful at it. However, he found that fame and fortune were not satisfying. "There was no long-term fulfillment in it," he says. "Something was missing."

He knew he wanted to do something great, he adds. Now, the church he founded is huge and he is using the Bible and the philosophy from his business background to "target the market." He states, "Old maps don't lead to new roads. If you want to travel on new roads, quit buying maps and start making maps."

Pastor Mike sees people in the trenches. He states, "Where you are isn't your destination, just your location." Using sound business practices with Biblical principles, he helps people achieve their full potential. Today, Pastor Mike has a bachelor's degree in Business and Accounting, a degree in Ministry with Greek, and a Master of Theology and is currently working on the completion of a Doctorate of Ministry in Pastoral Leadership. He says, "I am making new maps and living my dream."

ÿ *Pastor Michael Ware* ÿ

filé gumbo

Michael Ware, Pastor, Victory Church

Cajuns are known for their wonderful cuisine, especially gumbo. Here's a great dish that everyone will enjoy.

1 whole chicken

3/4 cups flour, for a dry roux

1 pound country sausage

louisiana hot sauce, not tabasco

1 large white onion

1-2 bunches green onions

1 small green bell pepper

worcestershire sauce

1 pound peeled shrimp cooked or uncooked

paul prudhomme's seafood magic, or cayenne pepper

garlic salt to taste or mrs. dash seasonings

filé for thickening

Cut the chicken into pieces and boil until cooked. De-bone the chicken and cut the meat into bite-sized pieces. Reserve the chicken stock; all of the ingredients will eventually be added to the stock.

To make the dry roux, it is important to brown the flour very slow in a cast-iron skillet. This process may take a few minutes, so make sure to not rush. Keep stirring continuously until the roux is browned to the color of light chocolate. The darker the roux is browned, the more robust the taste will be. Note, if the flour takes on a burned smell or presents any black flecks, you need to discard and start over. If the roux is burned, it will ruin the overall taste of the final product. Add the chicken stock and whisk to combine.

Slice the country sausage into small pieces. Brown the sausage in a skillet until the edges of the sausage are slightly blackened and crusted. Generously add Louisiana Hot Sauce while browning. When browned, add to the chicken stock/roux mixture. Finely chop the onion, bell pepper and the green onions, green tops and

(con't next column)

white portion, and cook in a cast-iron skillet for several minutes. Add water as necessary as well as generous amounts of Worcestershire Sauce to vegetables. Add this to the chicken stock/roux mixture. The aroma of the mixture should be very rich at this stage.

Add the shrimp and chicken to the mixture. Add the salt and/or season with the Paul Prudhomme's Seafood Magic to your individual taste. You can make it as spicy as you wish for a truly Cajun spicy flavor.

Last, begin adding filé (pronounced FEE-lay), which is made from the ground leaves of the sassafras tree, to the mixture until the gumbo thickens slightly. Serve in a bowl over steaming white rice, not instant rice. Add a little filé over the top to garnish and enhance the flavor. Enjoy the adventure of something different in every bite.

oven baked salmon

Georgy Kiss, Georgy's Station Break, Café International

Serves four. This salmon can be baked or grilled. This is an easy, light way to fix salmon.

1-1/2 cups soy sauce	Mix the soy sauce with the juice of the two limes.
2 medium limes	Place the salmon in the marinade. Cover and refrigerate for about four hours.
4 -6 ounces salmon fillet	
1 teaspoon olive oil	Spread the olive oil on a baking pan. Bake the salmon in 350-degree oven for twenty-to-thirty minutes.
	Serve with your favorite salad. Garnish with lemon and lime wedges.

red snapper vera cruz

Ian Kleinman, Executive Chef, Indigo Restaurant

3 pounds tomatoes, peeled

1 sweet red pepper, canned or fresh

**1 red snapper, approximately
four pounds**

2 tablespoons salt or to taste

3 tablespoons lime juice

4 tablespoons olive oil

1 large white onion, sliced thinly

15 pitted green olives

3 tablespoons large capers, drained

**6 canned whole chili largos or
canned jalapeños**

**1-1/2 tablespoons italian,
flat leaf parsley**

Seed and chop the tomatoes saving the seeds and peelings. Peel the red pepper and cut into strips. Rinse the fish well in cold water to remove any remaining scales. Pierce the flesh on both sides with a sharp fork and rub in the lime juice and about two teaspoons of the salt. Set the fish aside to season in an ovenproof dish in which the fish just fits. (If the dish is too large, the sauce will dry up.) Preheat oven to 350 degrees.

Heat the oil in a heavy frying pan. Add the onions and fry gently, stirring from time to time, until they are wilted but not browned. Add the chopped tomatoes. Press the seeds and pulp through a strainer to extract all the juice and combine with the olives, capers, half of the parsley and salt to taste. Cook over a fairly high flame until the sauce is well seasoned and reduced—about ten minutes. Pour the sauce over the fish. Cover the dish with foil and bake for twenty-five minutes.

Remove foil, turn the fish over and continue baking, uncovered, for twenty-five minutes or until fish is done. Baste with the sauce from time to time. When tested with a fork the flesh should flake easily away from the bone. Sprinkle with the rest of the parsley and decorate with the strips of red pepper. Serve the fish with plenty of the sauce and hot tortillas and/or white rice.

Tony Young's political career began at the Elbert County Commissioners in 1994 and led to serving as campaign aide for Mayor Hickenlooper. He also did a stint at the state house interning for Robert Hagedorn.

Tony says he learned Golden Rule principles early, listening, learning and imitating his father, who was a pastor for a Denver, Colorado church. "Growing up in that kind of an atmosphere was not easy," Tony says, "You were expected to act a certain way and you were always under the spotlight."

But his background was terrific training for being in the spotlight. Tony believes, "I live by the golden rule rather than the Machiavellian Rules of do to the other first." His gentle manner underscores the internal beliefs he has come to embrace. A father's influence does make a difference in the values one embraces.

When asked about his culinary interests he says, "I learned how to cook because my parents made me—so I would cook for myself and my family—but today, I do it because I like to eat and my recipes are straight from my mother."

tony's peppered shrimp

Tony Young, Aide to Mayor John Hickenlooper

For the beginner in the kitchen, this one is great to start cultivating culinary creations. Tony says he fixes this when he wants to be a little fancy.

1 yellow bell pepper

1 red bell pepper

1 yellow onion

4 cloves garlic, divided

salt to taste

pepper to taste

1/2 teaspoon dried oregano

1/2 pound peeled shrimp

1/2 pound scallops

1/2 stick butter

your favorite seasoning salt

cajun blackened seasoning salt

1/2 teaspoon dried dill weed

2 cups white rice

Cut peppers into strips and dice onion. Place all into frying pan with olive oil. Season the vegetables with two cloves garlic, salt, pepper and oregano. Sauté the vegetables until they are soft.

Rinse the shellfish in a colander under warm water. In a separate frying pan melt half a stick of butter. Add the shrimp and the scallops. Season the seafood with two cloves garlic, seasoning salt, blackened seasoning and dill weed. Once the seafood is cooked, add the vegetables to the mix.

Remove from heat. Place over a bed of hot rice and serve.

Ϋ Tony Young Ϋ

Stephen Kleinman, Executive Chef

Colorado Convention Center

Stephen Kleinman likens his job to the conductor of a large symphony orchestra. The 25,000-square-foot, on-site kitchen at the Colorado Convention Center can handle banquets for 2,400 in the ballroom and up to 15,000 on the exhibit floor. No problem for Stephen.

This chef apprenticed in Europe, graduated from the California Culinary Academy and left his stamp in Breckenridge, Colorado, establishing some twenty hotels and restaurants along the way. As a classic chef, his culinary palette includes tastes from French provincial to the Pacific Rim with a blended fusion of foods that makes his cuisine unique. Everything that passes through this kitchen is made from scratch.

Stephen's father owned restaurants and hotels in Norway. Both Stephen and his father were chef/instructors. Ian Kleinman, Stephen's son, learned culinary at the same time and place Stephen taught. So began a family culinary tradition.

❦ Stephen Kleinman ❦

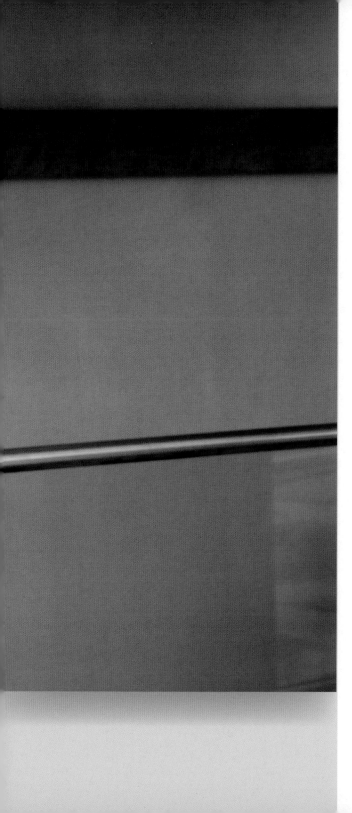

citrus salmon

Stephen S. Kleinman, Executive Chef, Colorado Convention Center

Serves four. This recipe goes nicely with Jasmine rice and pea pods.

4 oranges

4 limes

4 lemons

1 cup granulated sugar

2 cups water

24 ounces salmon

1 teaspoon sea salt

1/2 teaspoon white whole pepper

For citrus peelings: Peel the citrus fruit with a potato peeler. Place the peelings in a pot with one cup of sugar and two cups of water. Bring this to a boil and simmer for twenty minutes. Remove the peelings from the water and place them on a sheet pan. Warm them in a 200-degree oven until they are dried. Place the peelings in a blender and grind to a coarse consistency—or you can just chop with a knife. Set aside.

Squeeze the juice from the peeled fruit into a bowl and set aside. Season the salmon with salt and pepper and grill or bake lightly, about a couple of minutes, then cool. Dip the cool salmon in the citrus juices and then roll in the chopped citrus peelings.

To finish the salmon, cook in a 350-degree oven for twelve minutes, medium-rare, and serve.

easy cajun catfish

Amani Amir Ali, News Radio Clear Channel, 850 KOA

Feeds two or three people. Great Cajun taste. Add a little wine and atmosphere for a terrific light and quick meal.

1 cup brown or white rice

1 tablespoon tuscan lemon pepper olive oil

3-4 catfish fillets

old bay seasoning

2 cups water

louisiana cajun seasoning

1/2 pound fresh spinach leaves

Cook the rice in water with a tablespoon of Tuscan lemon-pepper olive oil according to the package directions.

Place the catfish in a preheated non-stick skillet. Oil is not needed because of the oil in the fish. Cook the fish at a slow heat until crispy, about ten minutes on each side. Dust each side with Old Bay Seasoning and the Louisiana Cajun seasoning. Don't over-season because a little goes a long way.

Place the dry, washed spinach leaves on a plate, spoon the hot rice in the center and top with a fish fillet.

Amani's famous Cajun Catfish is low-fat and melts in your mouth.

Both Amani Amir Ali and his wife, Gloria Neal, have careers well entrenched in the communications industry. Gloria is a news anchor for 850 KOA and Amani is a senior reporter. His international assignments took him into the villages of Bosnia and the Holy City of Mecca in Saudi Arabia. He served on broadcast management teams that work around the country including New Orleans where he converted to Islam.

He began his career in Washington, D.C., and went on to New Orleans. Besides the delectable delights he prepares in the kitchen, Ali keeps busy cooking up his journalistic magic to ensure the public stays well informed.

Determination has characterized Amani from the start. One pound, three ounces at birth, and not expected to live, Amani overcame those early odds. Today, his determination and fun-filled energy is evident to all who meet him. When not in the newsroom, Amani can be found in his kitchen preparing his famous Cajun Catfish, the cool jazz of Miles Davis sizzling the air. Ali says he learned his culinary secrets out of necessity. As a bachelor, grilled cheese sandwiches did very well, but Gloria's influence soon changed all that.

ÿ *Amani Amir Ali* ÿ

shrimp with lemon-garlic butter

James D. Saxton, Excel Services Network, Inc.

Jim suggests: "Serve the shrimp on brochettes as a first course or over your favorite fresh pasta as a main course. The lemon-garlic butter also works great with chicken breasts."

spice rub:

1 tablespoon sweet paprika

1 tablespoon garlic powder

1 teaspoon lemon pepper

2 teaspoons salt

24 large shrimp (1 pound), peeled and de-veined

lemon-garlic butter:

1/2 cup salted butter

finely grated zest of 1 lemon

juice of 1 lemon

3 cloves garlic, minced

1/2 teaspoon cayenne pepper

15 wooden skewers, soaked in water for 1/2 hour

Prepare the grill and oil the grill rack.

Make the spice rub by mixing together paprika, garlic powder, lemon pepper and salt in a small bowl. Coat the shrimp with the oil and sprinkle generously with the spice rub. Curl up one shrimp, tucking the tail end inside, and thread onto two parallel skewers. Repeat with the remaining shrimp, threading three-to-four shrimp on each pair of skewers.

For lemon butter: Melt the butter in a small saucepan over low heat. Stir in the lemon zest and juice, garlic and cayenne. Pour half of the lemon butter into a bowl to use for basting, keeping the rest warm.

Grill the shrimp directly over high heat, turning once and basting once or twice with the lemon-garlic butter, until it is evenly pink and opaque throughout, three-to-four minutes on each side. Do not overcook.

Transfer the skewers to a platter. Pour the reserved lemon-garlic butter over the shrimp and serve immediately.

oregano

thyme

simple salmon

Jon Tandler, Attorney at Law, Isaacson, Rosenbaum, Woods & Levy

Serves four with a half-pound of salmon per person. Jon suggests: "Instead of mayo use non-fat plain yogurt. You can do this dish on an outdoor grill and put the salmon on aluminum foil. This recipe also works well with red-meat trout."

2 pounds fresh salmon fillets	Place salmon in milk for thirty minutes, rinse and pat dry. Cover a cookie sheet with aluminum foil. Place salmon, skin-side down, on foil.
milk	
mayonnaise	Spread a thin layer of mayonnaise over salmon. Lightly season with garlic salt and then sprinkle generously with lemon pepper.
garlic salt	
lemon pepper	
fresh lemons	Broil at 500 degrees for five minutes. Reduce heat to 325 degrees for fifteen-to-twenty minutes.
	Use a spatula to remove salmon from the foil; leave the skin on the foil. Serve with lemons on the side.

Jon A. Winterton, Ph.D.

University of Colorado, Denver Center

Participating and learning from Dr. Jon Winterton is to invite a challenge in one's thinking and behavior. One of his many quotes: "I live on a two-way street; that which I do to others, they get to do to me. I treat my friends well and they treat me well."

As a professor in the sociology department at the University of Colorado, Denver Center, what Jon teaches is evidenced by the many lives he has influenced and is proof enough. His instruction is interesting with enlightened examples creating a lively, fun atmosphere. There are no dull moments in Professor Winterton's classroom.

He likes to say education is the process of creating a tolerance for uncertainty. That philosophy carries over to his cooking, where his experimentation has created wonderfully easy recipes, such as the Citrus Grilled Halibut, Sweet Cornish Game Hens and his Simple Chili Rellenos. Before his wife passed away in 1998, he was already handling the household cooking. Today, cooking for guests, the main course is friendly, inviting and satisfying, just like conversations with the professor himself.

℧ *Jon A. Winterton* ℧

citrus grilled halibut

Jon A. Winterton, Ph.D., University of Colorado, Denver Center

Serves four. The grapefruit side dish adds a nice, light touch for a great light meal.

1 cup soy sauce

1 lemon and 1 lime, juiced

pickled ginger

2 pounds halibut steak

1/2 cup mayonnaise

2 grapefruit

1/4 cup maple syrup

1 teaspoon butter, optional

Mix together the soy sauce, lemon and lime juice, and pickled ginger. Pour this over the halibut in a plastic bag and marinate for about two or three hours.

Just before grilling, cover the halibut with the mayonnaise to seal the fish. The mayonnaise burns off and will protect the flesh of the fish. Grill only a couple of minutes each side.

This goes well with baked grapefruit. Cut each grapefruit in half, take out the fruit and dice, and mix it with the maple syrup. Place the fruit back in the half shell and bake at 350 degrees for ten minutes. To make this richer, add a quarter teaspoon of butter per grapefruit half before baking.

Education is the process of creating a tolerance for uncertainty.

—Dr. Winterton

linguini with clams

Chef Mick Rosacci, Tony's Meats & Specialty Foods

Serves four. Use the clams from Tony's Meats for this recipe.

1/2 cup sea salt

16 -24 small, live clams

1/2 pound linguini

1/2 cup olive oil

1/2 onion, minced

2-4 garlic cloves, sliced

10-ounce can baby clams

1/2 cup clam juice

1/4 cup dry italian white wine

3 tablespoons italian parsley, minced

2 tablespoons fresh oregano, minced

2 tablespoons fresh thyme leaves

pinch of crushed red pepper

black pepper to taste

Dissolve one-half cup sea salt in two-to-three quarts of cold water to soak whole clams for approximately two hours; this cleans and purges them of their sand. Start pasta according to package directions.

In a large sauté pan, sauté onion and garlic in one-fourth cup oil until softened. Add wine, whole clams, clam juice, peppers and half of the fresh herbs. Boil, removing clams as they open. Reduce, taste and adjust sauce. Add canned clams and strained liquor if desired and heat through.

Add al dente pasta to the sauce, simmering and tossing. If sauce needs more liquid, splash with pasta water. Stir in clams, remove from heat and finish with pats of butter or a drizzle of flavorful olive oil. Toss in the remaining fresh chopped herbs and serve with lemon wedges, crusty bread and a tossed salad.

stir-fried scallops with asparagus

Ron Henderson, Denver Film Society

Serves four to six. Ron writes, "A Thai dish from my sister-in-law who lives in Singapore."

4 tablespoons vegetable oil, divided

1 bunch asparagus, cut into 2-inch lengths

4 garlic cloves, finely chopped

2 shallots, finely chopped

1 pound scallops

2 tablespoons fish sauce

1/2 teaspoon coarsely ground black pepper

1/2 cup coconut milk

coriander leaves for garnish

Heat half the oil in a wok or large frying pan. Add the asparagus and stir-fry for about two minutes. Transfer asparagus to a plate and set aside.

Add the rest of the oil, garlic and shallots to the same wok and fry until fragrant. Add the scallops and cook for another one or two minutes.

Return the asparagus to the wok. Add the fish sauce, black pepper and coconut milk.

Stir and cook for another three or four minutes or until the scallops and asparagus are cooked. Garnish with coriander leaves and serve.

cloves

pepper

shallots

Eric Chester,
Professional Speaker,
Author and President

Generation Why

Eric Chester is a specialist in kids. His company offers strategies for educating and employing the younger generation, dubbed Generation Why. From motivating at the speaker's platform to authoring eight books to consulting with major corporations, Eric Chester just simply believes in young people. If this sounds a little far-out, the kudos from Arbys, Dairy Queen, Universal Studios, ToysRUs and Little Caesars will make a believer out of you. Eric also has four of his own children.

When he's not writing sequels to his book, *TEEN POWER, a Treasury of Solid Gold Advice for Today's Teens by America's Top Youth Speakers, Trainers and Authors,* Eric also is a dynamite cook. Not surprisingly, the things he cooks up on the job are like his food: ingenious and meant to impact the people he touches.

ÿ *Eric Chester* ÿ

stuffed lake trout

Eric Chester, Generation Why

Serves four. Try this!

1 three-pound lake trout, dressed

1/4 cup lemon juice, divided

salt and pepper

2 cups dry bread crumbs

1 tablespoon dry dill weed

1/2 cup sour cream

1/2 teaspoon salt

few grinds of pepper corns

1 fresh lemon, cut in eighths

heavy-duty foil or
large covered roasting pan

Wash the lake trout in cold water and pat dry inside and out. Make long slashes every two inches about a quarter-inch deep through the skin along the body of the fish.

Sprinkle one-half the lemon juice in the cavity, and then sprinkle with the salt and pepper. Lay the trout on a sheet of heavy-duty foil that is slightly more than twice the length of the fish.

Combine the bread crumbs, dill weed, sour cream and a little salt and pepper. Stuff this mixture into the cavity. Bring edges of the foil together and seal well. Place on a sheet pan and roast in a 425-degree oven for ten minutes for each inch of thickness.

Remove from the oven and place on a serving platter. Open the foil and remove as much of the foil as possible—some may remain on the underside of the fish. (Most of the skin will adhere to the foil, remove any that does not stick to the foil.) Serve with fresh lemon wedges.

dill

Charlie Walling,
General Manager

Robinson Dairy

Charlie has spent twenty-two years in the dairy business and is currently the general manager of Robinson Dairy where he continues to keep the business on a successful path. He also uses his entrepreneurial talents within the community, serving on the board of directors of the Denver Chamber of Commerce Foundation, the Community College of Denver Foundation and Saint Joseph Hospital Foundation, and by developing and enhancing leadership in youth programs.

So, how does this "chef" find time to cook? As Charlie explains it, as a college student, cooking was a necessity. It certainly is cheaper than eating out and the food is better. As a husband and father, it was a natural transition. Like a lot of the men, they simply took over the task of cooking because it was there and they know how to do it well. Since Charlie knew how to cook, it became a hobby of his; he cooks two-to-three times per week.

tortilla-crusted shrimp with fettuccine in corn and poblano cream sauce

Charlie Walling, Robinson Dairy

Serves four. Robinson Dairy cream is the best for this recipe! For that extra-spicy flavor, use red chili-flavored fettuccine.

4 medium roasted poblano peppers

kernels from 2 ears corn

1 medium white onion, diced

4 serrano peppers, diced

3 tablespoons olive oil, divided

3 cups heavy cream

10 corn tortillas, pre-fried, or packaged tostadas, pre-fried

1 tablespoon cayenne

1 tablespoon dried caribe chili

12 large shrimp

1 cup flour

2 eggs beaten

2 cups canola oil

12 ounces, al dente fettuccine

12 sprigs fresh cilantro for garnish

Place poblano peppers on a cookie sheet or tray and broil in preheated oven until charred and puffy, turning frequently. Wrap in paper towels for ten minutes. Skin should remove easily.

For the corn and poblano cream sauce: In a large sauté pan, sauté onion and serrano peppers in two tablespoons olive oil over medium heat. When mixture becomes soft, add corn and poblano peppers and continue to sauté for an additional two minutes. Add the cream and simmer for fifteen minutes.

Pour the entire mixture into a blender and briefly puree until smooth. Pour sauce through a strainer into a saucepan, pushing solids with a spoon to extract as much liquid as possible, and keep warm until needed.

To make the Tortilla Crusted Shrimp: Crush the fried tortillas into very small pieces and add cayenne and dried Caribe Chili, set aside. Dredge cleaned and de-veined shrimp in the flour. Dip in beaten eggs, coat with tortilla breading. Place in hot oil in a medium sauté pan and fry for two-to-three minutes, turning with tongs once. Remove and place on paper towel until needed.

Cook the fettuccine al dente. Drain and toss with one tablespoon of olive oil. Place pasta on four warm plates, ladle sauce over the pasta, place three shrimp around the pasta on each plate and garnish each with three sprigs of cilantro.

ÿ *Charlie Walling* ÿ

great chicken, turkey & fowl

echo hunt club pheasant on the barbie • crusted chicken • steve's huevos rancheros • simply delicious shrimp-covered chicken crepes • ortiz chicken enchiladas • coconut basil chicken • sweet cornish game hens • szechuan chicken tacos • chicken pasta marinara • low-fat chicken fajitas • chicken chili lasagna • glazed jalapeño jelly chicken • tequila lime breast with pico de gallo • grilled chicken provolone • scottish chicken tikka marsala

Scott Cortelyou, Anchor Man

Business for Breakfast, Clear Channel 760 AM

As co-anchor with TJ Maxwell on KKZN's 760, The Zone, Scott sounds out the trumpet beat of market trends, keeping listeners in tune with the bells of the hottest stocks. He got his training as a morning disc jockey in high school, running a radio station in the wee hours before heading off to school each day.

Now he daily keeps his listeners abreast of market trends but at night he turns into Emeril the Second. Married to a busy computer specialist for Remax Int'l, he admits, "Cooking was the one thing I could do to offset her long tedious hours."

When asked which cookbook is his favorite, Scott's response was, "The three-ring binder that holds my own recipes, of course." This eclectic, delightful recipe book holds the secrets of many a meal that eventually became his array of culinary specialties.

ÿ *Scott Cortelyou* ÿ

echo hunt club pheasant
on the barbie

Scott Cortelyou, Business for Breakfast, Clear Channel, 760 AM

Scott hunts his own pheasants. After much trial and error he has found this a good way to prepare them. With pheasants, he says, there isn't much else but the breast meat.

3 pheasant-breast fillets, cut into bite-size pieces

1 large onion, cut into same size

1 large bell pepper, cut same

1 pound bacon, each strip cut into thirds

cavender's greek spice mix

Chop the pheasant, onion and bell pepper into bite-size pieces.

Wrap each piece of pheasant with the bacon, alternate placing them on shish-kebob skewers, with the vegetables.

Sprinkle liberally with Cavender's Greek Spice mix. Grill over medium coals, only until bacon is done. With some grills, a piece of aluminum foil between the kebobs and the coals helps prevent flare-ups.

Serve as appetizer or entree, depending on crowd size and amount of bird meat on hand.

crusted chicken

Eric Chester, Generation Why

This is a version of fried chicken that's grilled, not fried!

for marinade:

1/4 cup orange marmalade

1/4 cup orange juice

2 tablespoons soy sauce

1 teaspoon fresh ginger root, grated

1-1/2 teaspoons dijon mustard

1 garlic clove, minced

3-1/2 pounds skinless chicken thighs

1 cup lightly crushed corn flakes

for salsa:

4 california peaches, chopped

1/2 cup orange marmalade

1/2 cup green onions, thinly sliced

2 tablespoons cider vinegar

1 teaspoon fresh ginger root, grated

In a small bowl, combine the first six ingredients to make an orange-ginger marinade. Place the chicken in a zip-top plastic bag. Pour marinade over the chicken; close the bag securely, turning to coat well. Refrigerate for two hours.

Remove the chicken from the marinade and roll in the corn flakes. Pat extra corn flakes on if necessary to make a solid coating. Place the chicken in lightly oiled disposable aluminum foil pan; cover loosely with foil. Cook on covered grill over medium heat thirty-to-forty minutes or until cooked through. Uncover for the last ten minutes.

Tangy Peach Salsa: Combine peaches, marmalade, green onions, vinegar and ginger root in a medium bowl. Refrigerate until ready to use. Makes two-and-one-half cups.

Serve chicken hot or cold with the salsa.

One-quarter teaspoon dried ginger can be substituted for the fresh ginger. Also, the chicken can be baked in a conventional oven at 350 degrees for thirty-to-forty minutes.

steve's huevos rancheros

Steven H. Lutton, Renegade Press

Serves six. Your weekend guests would enjoy this or serve it at a Sunday brunch.

1 small can refried beans

1 tablespoon olive oil

1 cup shredded cheddar cheese, divided

6 soft flour tortillas

1 dozen eggs

1/2 teaspoon garlic powder

1 cup sour cream

1 cup steve's tomato salsa (see page 99) or use your favorite

Combine beans, olive oil, garlic powder and one-quarter cup shredded cheddar in small pan. Heat to a simmer.

Spread the beans over tortillas. Sprinkle with a half-cup of cheddar. Broil until bubbly. While heating, fry eggs to over-easy.

Place two eggs on one-half of tortilla, fold other half over. Sprinkle a little cheese on top and put back into broiler. Toast until slightly brown and remove. Spread sour cream over the top. Top with the salsa. Enjoy!

simply delicious shrimp-covered chicken crepes

Eric Kloverstrom, Partner & Director of Operations, J&W Wholesale Distribution, LLC

Serves four to six. For the crepes, see Steve Kelley's Crepes on page 180.

2 tablespoons olive oil

1/2 cup onions, chopped

4–6 chicken breasts cut into 1/4-inch strips

1/2 cup table cream

3 cups chicken broth, divided

1-1/4 cups clam juice, divided

1/2 teaspoon konriko-brand creole seasoning

1/4 cup onions, minced

4 tablespoons cornstarch, divided

salt to taste

2 cloves garlic, crushed

1/2 cup parmesan and romano cheese combination

1 pound popcorn shrimp, pre-cooked and de-veined

dash paprika

8–12 crepes, recipe on page 180

1 two-ounce jar capers

For the chicken filling: Sauté the half-cup of onions in olive oil. Add the chicken and brown. Cover and continuing cooking on low for thirty minutes or until the chicken is done.

Combine one cup of the chicken broth and two tablespoons cornstarch; add the three-fourths cup clam juice. Pour into the chicken mixture and heat, stirring until the whole mixture is thickened and bubbly. Add the Creole seasoning and salt to taste. Keep the filling warm while preparing the shrimp topping sauce.

For the shrimp sauce: Sauté the minced onions and crushed garlic. Combine two tablespoons cornstarch with two cups of chicken broth and a half cup of clam juice. Add the cream. Pour into the minced onion pan and bring to a boil, stirring while it thickens.

Add the cream and cheese. Heat until the cheese melts into the mixture. Add the shrimp and heat; remove immediately so the shrimp are not overcooked.

Fill the crepes with the chicken mixture; fold over and top with the shrimp sauce. Sprinkle a few capers on top with a lace of paprika for color and serve. Enjoy!

Note: More thickening can be added to the chicken and shrimp sauce if a thicker consistency is desired.

Eric Kloverstrom, Sales Associate

Cole Harford

To know Eric Kloverstrom is to see the gentle spirit that resides within this talented man. As a beginning trumpet player in grade school, his band instructor singled him out as someone who had a natural ability and who one day would make his trumpet sizzle. Eric went on to graduate from Colorado Christian University in 1998 with a music performance minor and a marketing major, and is now partner and director of operations for J&W Wholesale Distribution, a distributor of paper products for restaurants and institutions.

Not only is this gentleman a terrific musician, he also knows how to cook. But, did this gentleman learn his culinary pursuits watching his mother slave away at their country home? Absolutely not! Rather, he began working at the B & B Cafe in Castle Rock, starting as a dishwasher and working his way up to cook. Angie Loiacono, his boss, is the one who is responsible for his culinary pursuits.

Many summers and weekends were spent on this job, which helped pay bills while he went to school. Some of his friends found out his talent, and soon enlisted him to cater for their rehearsal dinners before their weddings. Rumor is, he has even cooked a dinner or two for an occasional date.

ÿ *Eric **K**loverstrom* ÿ

Joshua Phillip Ortiz

Growing up in a small town, Josh Ortiz learned early the value of things and the importance of a close family. He learned how to cook from his mom and dad, taking recipes, experimenting with them, and creating his own culinary masterpieces. Today he cooks for his bride, family and friends.

Josh Ortiz says staying physically fit is an important life choice. Practicing what he preaches, Josh has run the Bolder Boulder in fifty-one minutes. He and his wife love to work out; his wife is his motivation to keeping physically fit. In fact that he was born on Thanksgiving Day at the same time the Broncos were playing didn't hurt.

ÿ Joshua Ortiz ÿ

ortiz chicken enchiladas

Joshua Phillip Ortiz

Serves four to six. A pound of ground beef can be substituted for the chicken or simply use the cheese for cheese enchiladas.

1 whole chicken

2 tablespoons oil

2 tablespoons flour

3 tablespoons red chili powder or enchilada powder

1 cup water

1 eight-ounce can tomato sauce

1/4 teaspoon garlic powder

1 teaspoon cumin

2 cloves garlic, chopped

1/2 onion, chopped

1 package of twelve corn tortillas

1-1/2 cups grated cheddar cheese

Boil a whole chicken or cook in a crockpot until done. De-bone the meat and shred.

Heat oil on medium heat and add the flour and brown. Mix in the red chili powder, water, tomato sauce, garlic powder, cumin, chopped garlic and onion.

Soak individual corn tortillas in the sauce mixture until slightly soft. Make layers of soaked corn tortillas, chicken and cheese in a covered casserole pan. Bake at 350 degrees until cheese melts. Serve and enjoy.

joshua ortiz
joshua ortiz
joshua
ortiz

coconut basil chicken

Dom Testa, MIX 100 Radio

Serves about four. Dom says:"I love cooking with a wok and somehow find a way to do it at least once a week. This recipe can be made in another large pan, but for goodness sake, if you don't have a wok, go get one right now!"

1-1/2 to 2 pounds boneless, skinless chicken breasts

3-4 tablespoons olive oil

1 medium onion, chopped

3-4 cloves garlic, minced

2 tablespoons ginger

2-3 ounces diced green chilies

3/4 cup coconut milk

1/4 cup soy sauce

2 tablespoons distilled white vinegar

1 cup fresh basil

1 medium green bell pepper, slivered

rice

Cut the chicken into small strips, approximately one inch by one-quarter inch. Set this aside in a bowl.

Coat the bottom of wok or large pan with olive oil and heat. Add the onion, garlic, ginger and diced chilies. Stir frequently and cook until the onion is slightly browned. Spoon the mixture out of the wok and set it aside in a bowl.

Add the chicken strips to the wok and cook, stirring until lightly browned. Remove from the wok and set aside in a bowl.

Pour coconut milk, soy sauce and vinegar into the wok. Bring to a boil until slightly reduced, five-to-six minutes. Pour the onion mixture and chicken into the wok and coat with the sauce. Add the basil and bell pepper and heat. Serve over rice.

Dominic (Dom) Testa, Anchor Man

MIX 100 Radio, Dom & Jane

"Creatively wild," "innovatively up-to-date" and "latest trends" describe the Big MIX Morning Show on MIX 100 Radio, more commonly known as the Dom & Jane Show. Dom Testa, still going strong as host for more than ten years, entertains his audience with wit, charm and humor.

When asked why he started cooking, he says point-blank, "My dad is a fantastic cook. It must be in the genes."

Listening to his shows, which now number well over 11,000, is an upbeat experience. You end up feeling that you know Dom personally, listening to his comments about his wife, Beverly, his son, Dominic III, and Syd the cat, commonly known as Monkey Butt.

ẏ Dom Testa ẏ

sweet cornish game hens

Jon A. Winterton, Ph.D., University of Colorado, Denver Center

Serves four. This is a delightfully quick, easy meal. Dr. Winterton has a host of original recipes to make delicious dinners.

2 cornish game hens

2 tablespoons sea salt

1 teaspoon lemon pepper

1 cup orange juice concentrate

2 acorn squash, halved

1/4 cup maple syrup

Cover the Cornish game hens with a mixture of water, sea salt and lemon pepper and marinate for one-to-two hours. Take the hens out of the marinade and place them in a baking dish; salt and pepper to taste with sea salt and lemon pepper.

Bake the hens covered at 350 degrees for one hour. Five minutes before taking them out of the oven, baste the hens with the orange concentrate. This only needs five minutes, and will add an excellent flavor. Serve immediately.

Acorn squash: The game hens go well with acorn squash. Seed them and place, cut side down, in about a half inch of water and the maple syrup. Place the squash in the oven the same time as the Cornish game hens for a terrifically easy, quick meal.

Tip: Turkey also can be cooked with the orange concentrate; about fifteen minutes before taking the turkey out of the oven, take out the stuffing and coat the surface with the orange concentrate.

szechuan chicken tacos

Stephen Kleinman, Executive Chef, Colorado Convention Center

Serves four. This dish is well worth the effort in creating the accompanying side dishes. For serving to company, make the corn relish and black bean salsa ahead. Use some of the more unusual mushrooms for a richer taste.

3/4 pound boneless, skinless chicken breasts, cubed

1/2 cup olive oil, divided

2 teaspoons minced ginger

2 teaspoons granulated garlic

2 ounces shiitake mushrooms, sliced

1/2 teaspoon szechuan pepper

1-1/2 cups white wine

1 cup hoisin sauce

12 corn tortillas

mixed greens

black bean salsa, page 116

corn relish, page 117

cilantro and radish sprouts to garnish

12-20 enoki mushrooms

In a wok, heat two tablespoons oil and sauté chicken until lightly browned. Add ginger and garlic.

Add shiitake mushrooms and Szechuan pepper; deglaze with wine. Stir in hoisin sauce and cook until sauce thickens.

In two large sauté pans, heat remaining oil. Take each tortilla and fill with equal parts of the chicken mix. Fold the tacos in half and sauté each side until crispy. If six tacos won't fit in each pan, cook in smaller batches, holding cooked tacos in warm oven.

On each of four plates, place mixed greens in a strip across center of plate. On the left, place a spoonful of salsa, and on the right a spoonful of relish. Fill each taco with sprouts and lay three in a row on top of greens, garnishing the first taco with three enoki mushrooms.

Steve Gottsegen, Sports Anchor

KMGH TV-7

For Steve Gottsegen, cooking has always meant cooking nutritious meals to keep weight off and stay in shape. He also keeps in shape by spending time off playing in a local football league, golfing, working out and skiing in the winter. However, if you get a chance to look up to his second-story balcony, you might just see him barbecuing some sizzling mouth-watering goodies for that special someone. Wonder who that could be?

Steve grew up in Denver and attended Thomas Jefferson High School and Colorado State University, where he proved his own athletic skills on the pitcher's mound. Interesting to note, childhood classmates today are surprised to see Steve as a sportscaster; he was one of those shy, quiet types who kept to himself for the most part and didn't say a lot. But, he certainly has made up for that today.

chicken pasta marinara

Steve Gottsegen, KMGH TV 7

Steve does not use canned tomatoes unless he is in a hurry. For him, fresh is always best. He says, "I am not a salt kind of a guy…but I'm rare." Steve loves to grill.

1/4 cup olive oil

7-8 cloves sliced garlic

3-4 large tomatoes, crushed

1 small can tomato paste

1 teaspoon basil

1 teaspoon oregano

1/4 cup red wine

1/4 cup chopped onion browned

1/2 cup chopped red and green pepper

salt to taste

pepper to taste

2 large chicken breasts

your favorite pasta

Brown the garlic cloves in the olive oil over medium heat.

Stir in crushed tomatoes, tomato paste, onions, wine, spices and seasonings. Bring to boil. Then let simmer on low for about twenty-five minutes.

Grill the chicken. No additional spices are necessary, but do what you want.

Cut the grilled chicken into chunks, and then stir them into the sauce along with the red and green peppers.

Once pasta is ready, spoon out the chicken and sauce over the pasta and enjoy a low-fat, delicious, and easy meal.

low-fat chicken fajitas

Steve Gottsegen, KMGH TV-7

Steve says:"I always go with fat-free when possible. But you can make this as low-fat or high-fat as you like. It's quick, delicious, and the cleanup isn't bad at all."

1 pound chicken strips or steak strips

1/2 cup chopped onions

1/2 teaspoon black pepper

1/2 teaspoon chili pepper

1/2 teaspoon garlic powder

1/2 teaspoon oregano

1 tablespoon olive oil

1/4 cup sliced green peppers

1/4 cup sliced red peppers

1 avocado, sliced

add:

low-fat tortillas

fat-free sour cream

fat-free cheese

salsa of your choice

Brown the chicken or steak in olive oil. Throughout the process add in the spices, onions and a little bit of water to keep everything moist and not smoking.

Add peppers when fajitas are two-to-three minutes from being ready. If you put them in too early they get soggy, and I like them crunchy. But the earlier you put them in the softer they'll get.

Put tortillas in tin foil and heat in the oven at 350 degrees for about five-to-seven minutes to soften and warm. And, that's it.

chicken and chili lasagna

Eric Chester, Generation Why

This dish has been described as surprisingly good. Make sure the cream cheese is soft for easy spreading.

6 ounces cream cheese, softened

1 medium onion, chopped

8 green onions, chopped

2 cups, shredded mexican-cheese blend

2 cloves garlic

3/4 teaspoon ground cumin, divided

1/2 teaspoon minced fresh cilantro or parsley

3 cups cooked chicken

1/4 cup butter or margarine

1/4 cup all-purpose flour

1-1/2 cups chicken broth

1 cup shredded monterey jack cheese

1 cup sour cream

1 tablespoon fresh thyme

1 four-ounce can chopped green chilies, drained

1/8 teaspoon each salt & pepper

12 six-inch halved flour tortillas

In a mixing bowl, combine cream cheese, onions, one-and-a-half cups Mexican-cheese blend, garlic, one-fourth teaspoon cumin and cilantro. Stir in chicken and set aside.

In a saucepan, melt butter. Stir in the flour until smooth; gradually add the broth. Bring to a boil, cook and stir for two minutes or until thickened.

Remove from the heat; stir in the Monterey Jack cheese, sour cream, a little thyme, chilies, salt, pepper and remaining cumin.

Spread half of the cheese sauce in a greased 13"x 9" x 2" baking dish. Top with six tortilla halves, a third of the chicken mixture and a fourth of the cheese sauce.

Repeat tortilla, chicken and cheese sauce layers twice. Top with the remaining tortillas, cheese sauce and Mexican cheese.

Cover and bake at 350 degrees for thirty minutes. Uncover; bake ten minutes longer or until heated through. Let stand five minutes before cutting.

glazed jalapeño jelly chicken

Dick Lewis, The Richard's Agency

This easy recipe goes well with a corn and lima bean succotash. Add a teaspoon of basil to the succotash while cooking. ENJOY!

1 heaping teaspoon jalapeños, finely chopped

3 heaping tablespoons dijon mustard

4 tablespoons lemon juice, fresh or concentrate

1/2 jar of hot jalapeño jelly

4 half chicken breasts, pounded until thickness is even

salt and pepper to taste

4 medium celery stalks, cut julienne style

In a bowl, mix chopped jalapeños, mustard, lemon juice and jalapeño jelly. Heat in a medium microwave for about a minute or less and stir. Set aside.

Season both sides of the chicken breasts with salt and black pepper.

In a large skillet cook the chicken breasts topped with half the jelly mixture on medium high for about four minutes.

Turn and add celery sticks to pan and coat the other side with the remaining jelly mixture. Put some of the celery on top as well. Cook until done.

Tell em Dick Lewis sent you!

Ÿ Dick Lewis Ÿ

Dick Lewis, Co-Owner

The Richard's Agency

Remember the Mickey Mouse Club? It debuted in July 1955, and ran 360 episodes over the next three years. Dick Lewis was the MC of the local version of the Mickey Mouse Club on Denver's Channel 9 (then known as KBTV). At 6:30 a.m. he would bring children into daily activities with morning cartoons and then be back in the afternoon to greet them with his version of the Mickey Mouse Club.

If that doesn't jog the memory, what about: "Tell 'em Dick Lewis sent you!" Yes, as a popular commercial pitchman, his classy showmanship sold goods for businesses like Uncle Bob Porter's Rebuilt Engines. Is this unclogging the old memory banks?

Now Dick is "retired" and at seventy-seven is a partner in an ad agency promoting businesses like Bud's Mufflers, Hickory Baked Hams and Gnat Original Design Jewelers in Cherry Creek North. "Twenty-six years ago I stopped eating red meat, salt, sugar, grease, butter or margarine," he says, "and I feel better, look good and am the only male who lived past forty-four in my family." Oh yes, he quit smoking as well.

ꙮ *Georgy Kiss* ꙮ   ꙮ *SteveKelley* ꙮ

tequila lime chicken breast with pico de gallo

Georgy Istran Kiss, Georgy's Station Break, Café International

Serves four. This is a great quick meal and also a great recipe for the culinary novice.

4 six-ounce chicken breasts

1-1/2 cups soy sauce

2 medium limes

1/2 cup tequila

pinch black pepper

pinch granulated garlic

for pico de gallo:

1 bunch cilantro

1 jalapeño

1 large tomato

1 bunch scallions

1 medium lime

pinch salt

Mix the soy sauce, juice from the two limes, tequila, pepper and garlic.

Cover the chicken with the mixture and marinate for three-to-four hours.

Place the chicken in a pan and bake at 350 degrees for twenty-to-thirty minutes or until done.

Serve with rice, black beans and Pico de Gallo.

For the Pico de Gallo: Wash the cilantro and chop the leaves.

Dice the tomatoes and jalapeño. Slice the scallions.

Mix all the vegetables with juice from the lime and salt.

This is great with the chicken breasts, but also goes well with salads.

Georgy Kiss, Hungarian Chef

Café International Catering, Clear Channel

Georgy Kiss discovered his culinary interests serendipitously as a soldier in the Hungarian army. He had been sent to KP duty as punishment for breaking their rules, but while he was there, he found his inner passion. Grabbing the opportunity while on KP duty, Georgy bribed a clerk and received a three-month culinary training on the basics of dealing with a large kitchen.

Before the army, however, to sooth family pressure, he had become a tailor. The traditional mindset was that you could do nothing and go nowhere as a cook! But, like a true artist, he decided to follow his dream and eventually enrolled in a four-year course at the Culinary Institute of Hungary.

Seeking a better life, Georgy then fled Hungary in 1981, following his brother to Denver. He thought that he would stay a few months; he has been here ever since. Note: Clear Channel personnel think they have the best cafeteria in Denver.

Steve Kelley's profile is page 181.

Richard Kemerling, Owner

Prime-Sight Associates, dba Pearle Vision

Richard Kemerling is a man dedicated to his family, who has an appreciation of the wild and an enjoyment of good friends. But dedication to good eats? He admits that he once declared his culinary desire as a way to get out of clean-up detail as a Boy Scout. Learning to cook on the trail back then was good training, though.

Married twenty-three years to his wife, Kae, they have a son and a daughter. Richard is described as a compassionate conservative who learned appreciation for the environment during those treks in the wild as a Scout. Today Richard does all of the family meal preparation. "Cooking alleviates the burden from Kae," he says, "We each have our own household duties. Dinner is a family event where we come together to connect."

Richard's recipes are his own culinary creations; ingenuity sparks his imagination as he refines and cultivates new recipes. However, he adds, "I don't cook anything that takes longer to make than to eat." This Denver Man in the Kitchen has enough original recipes stashed away to write his own book: quick and wholesome, great idea.

As owner of Prime-Sight Associates, and having a degree in Ophthalmic Optics, Richard is aware of how good nutrition affects other areas of good health, including good eyesight.

ॐ **Richard Kemerling** ॐ

grilled chicken provolone

Richard Kemerling, Prime-Sight Associates, dba Pearle Vision

Serves four. This is one of those meals that can be done in a few moments, leaving time for the enjoyment of company.

4 boneless chicken breasts

1-2 cups favorite italian salad dressing

8 slices canadian bacon

4 slices provolone cheese

Flatten chicken breasts and place in a large baking dish. Cover and marinate chicken breasts in salad dressing overnight in the refrigerator.

Prepare your grill for direct heat. Lightly grill the Canadian bacon rounds on both sides and remove from the grill.

Grill chicken breasts over direct heat until first side is nicely seared. Turn breasts and sear other side for one-to-two minutes.

Brush breasts with remaining salad dressing. Place one provolone cheese round, folded in half, on top of each chicken breast and place two Canadian bacon rounds on top of the cheese.

Reduce the heat and cook under covered grill until the cheese has melted. Remove breasts and garnish with your favorite Italian seasoning. Serve with pasta and Italian salad.

Note: For each additional serving, add one breast and appropriate cheese and bacon.

"You either learned how to cook well or you got dunked."

—*Richard Kemerling*

Martin Faith, Owner & Designer

Scottish Stained Glass Corporation

Take the artist out of the studio, but never take the studio out of the artist. Talent will find its way in all of us, and so it is with this Scottish immigrant. Though his degree is in economics, he's always had a love for art. "Discovery of stained glass along with my background in economics has combined the best of both worlds," he says. So, how does cooking connect with this designer entrepreneur?

"At the age of twelve," he adds, "it was just my dad, my brother and me. We all took turns cooking. I could cook anything I wanted when it was my turn."

When Martin and his wife, Gillian, came to the United States in 1991, they discovered Indian food was a rarity here. Scotland, on the other hand, is filled with Indian establishments where people wait an hour for a table. So, Martin took up Indian cuisine. Today, he not only cooks awesome Indian food, but also uses cooking as a way to release stress and to let out more of those creative juices.

ÿ *Martin Faith* ÿ

chicken tikka

2-1/2 pounds thawed chicken tenders
12 ounces plain yogurt
1 teaspoon salt
1 teaspoon paprika
1 teaspoon chili powder
3 tablespoons oil
3 drops red food color

Combine all the chicken tikka ingredients, mix well and refrigerate for a minimum of two hours. After marinating, cook on the grill or hot oven.

scottish chicken tikka masala

Martin Faith, Scottish Stained Glass

Serves six to eight. Tikka traditionally is an Indian dish of marinated meat cooked on a skewer. The chicken tikka is served in a sauce over Basmati rice.

previous page, chicken tikka

1 pound onions, peeled and chopped

1 ounce garlic, chopped

1 ounce fresh ginger root, peeled and chopped in small pieces

1 teaspoon salt

1 pint water

4 tablespoons vegetable oil

1/2 teaspoon turmeric

1/2 teaspoon chili powder

1 teaspoon paprika

2 tablespoons tomato paste

1/2 pound mushrooms, chopped

1 fourteen-ounce can tomatoes, peeled and chopped

1-1/2 teaspoon garam masala

1/2 teaspoon ground cumin

1 tablespoon dried fenugreek leaves

1 teaspoon dried cilantro

1 tablespoon lemon juice

3/4 cup table cream

2 tablespoons fresh chopped cilantro

For the sauce: Combine the onions, garlic, salt and water in a pan. Bring to a boil and cook for forty-five minutes. Remove from heat and set aside to cool. In a clean pan, heat oil, turmeric, chili powder, paprika and tomato paste. Cook for two minutes, stirring constantly.

In a blender, put half the can of tomatoes and liquify. Add this to the pan and cook for five minutes. Turn the heat down, add the garam masala, lemon juice, cumin, fenugreek, mushrooms, dried cilantro, and the remainder of the can of tomatoes. Cover and simmer for one hour.

Cut each of the cooked chicken tenders into two or three pieces and add to the sauce, along with the lemon juice. Cook for an additional three minutes.

Stir in the cream and serve over Basmati rice. Sprinkle chopped cilantro on the top and serve.

mighty & meaty

menudo • grilled veal chop with wild mushroom ragout • roasted loin of colorado lamb with thyme merlot sauce • ham loaf • baked steak • firehouse pork chops • grandma rosie's sunday sauce • grandpa seno's meatballs • beef bourguignonne • osso buco with pine nut gremolata • zippy pepper-jack breakfast casserole • brown veal sauce • lamb stock • dilbeck's denver ribs • beef tenderloin stuffed with garlic

Craig Peña, Designer

Chingaso Gear and Suavecito Apparel Company

Embracing one's past is often the path to profitable situations. So it is with Craig Peña. As co-owner of Suavecito Apparel Company and the Chingaso Gear clothing line, Craig seeks the quality of life that comes with cultivating family and friends. Sometimes he cooks for a hundred people or more.

"My mom could make something out of nothing," he recalls. He was age eight when he started making lunches for her. "I wanted to have a hot meal for the two of us; I would start the beans." He also would sit at the feet of his aunts and learn from their culinary successes. Now they ask him about his.

Craig's business acumen began at a young age as well. As a teen, he purchased clothing at the thrift store and remade them to fit. That led to creating his own line of clothing.

Craig and his partner, Jay Salas, have been featured twice on the front page of the New York Times style section, among others, and their outfits are worn by such notables as Snoop Dog, Garth Brooks and Mayor John Hickenlooper.

menudo

Craig Robert Peña, Chingaso Gear and Suavecito Apparel Company

Feeds approximately thirty-to-fifty people, depending on their hunger. This original recipe suits Craig's life style of lots of family and friends. You can pick up the tripe and patas at your local carniceria.

2 pounds patas (pigs feet)

1-1/2 cans (102 ounces) hominy

2 medium yellow onions

3 tablespoons chopped garlic

1 pound or so mild-to-medium powdered red chili

about 1/2 cup oregano

1/4 - 1/3 cup of salt

10 pounds honey-combed tripe

At one time Craig was a social worker in the Bronx, working with AIDS patients, and helping provide residential services for formally homeless mentally ill people.

Fill a three-gallon stockpot approximately one-third full of water. Drain the hominy and place in the pot. Dice the onions and place in the pot. In fact, put everything but the tripe into the pot and bring to a boil.

Cut the tripe into one-inch squares or slightly smaller and place in a colander. Rinse the pieces pretty well and add to the stockpot. Top off the stockpot with water. Bring everything to a boil, then reduce to simmer. Simmer overnight or for about ten-to-twelve hours—more if you'd like.

For garnish: Serve with a garnish of diced onions, oregano, chili piquin and lemon wedges; some people like shredded cheese on top also.

Helpful Hints: Cut up the tripe when it's still partially frozen (it usually comes frozen). Otherwise it's kind of like trying to cut slimy shoe leather. As for the salt, it seems like a lot, however, the hominy absorbs it for the most part. Start out with a bit under one-fourth cup and then taste and add more if needed after about four hours of cooking. As with all my recipes, season to your tastes!

ÿ **Craig Peña** ÿ

grilled veal chop with wild mushroom ragout

Mark Black, Executive Chef, Brown Palace Hotel

Yields eight servings. To french the chops, cut the meat away from the bone.

for ragout:

3 ounces bacon, diced

1 tablespoon minced garlic

1 tablespoon minced shallots

1 cup leeks, sliced thin

1 pint peeled pearl onions

1 tablespoon fresh thyme, chopped

12 ounces assorted wild mushrooms, chopped

1 pint white wine

1 quart brown veal sauce, page 84

8 veal chops, frenched, 10 ounces each

4 ounces olive oil

salt & pepper to taste

4 roma tomatoes, diced

For the Wild Mushroom Ragout: render the bacon in a saucepot. Add the garlic, shallots, leeks, onions and thyme and sauté until tender. Add the mushrooms and sauté for five minutes. Deglaze with the white wine and simmer for ten-to-fifteen minutes.

Add the Brown Veal Sauce and reduce to the desired consistency, approximately fifteen minutes.

Meanwhile, brush the veal chops with olive oil and season with salt and pepper. Grill over a hot grill to the desired doneness.

To the Wild Mushroom Ragout add the diced tomatoes and salt and pepper to taste.

Arrange each chop with side dishes as desired, top with the Wild Mushroom Ragout.

Mark Black, Executive Chef

Brown Palace Hotel

While all of the men in *Denver Men in the Kitchen* are gifted, not all are "weekend" chefs and closet cooks. Some make their living at it—and do it very well. As the executive chef for the Brown Palace Hotel, Mark Black oversees seven sous chefs and fifty cooks responsible for five restaurants, including the four-star Palace Arms, 24-hour room service, catered events and the famous Lobby Tea. He also has made appearances at the prestigious James Beard House in New York, and appearances on CBS's Early Show "Chef on a Shoestring" and numerous Food Network shows.

Chef Black also is a contributor to "On Cooking," a food textbook used by over 300 culinary programs. He serves on the Advisory Committee for the Art Institute of Colorado, as an Education Fund board member for the Colorado Restaurant Association, and as a mentor for the Culinary Institute of America.

His passion for cooking and good food carries over into his personal life as well. His favorite meals served to family and friends encompass many cuisines, and are stand-outs with fresh, quality ingredients.

thyme merlot sauce

Sauté the garlic and shallots in the clarified butter until translucent.

Add the wine, bay leaf and thyme and simmer until reduced by half.

Add the stock and reduce by half again, strain and season to taste

roasted loin of colorado lamb with thyme merlot sauce

Mark Black, Executive Chef, Brown Palace Hotel

Serves eight. This recipe goes along with the Brown Palace tradition of excellence when it comes to fine dining.

1/4 teaspoon garlic, minced

1 teaspoon shallots, minced

1 tablespoon clarified butter

8 ounces merlot wine

1 laurel bay leaf

1 teaspoon fresh thyme, chopped

20 ounces lamb stock, page 85

salt & pepper to taste

4 lamb loins, boneless & trimmed

12 ounces thyme merlot sauce

Season the lamb loins with salt and pepper. Sear the lamb in hot oil in a sauté pan. Transfer the pan to a 325-degree oven and roast to medium rare. Remove from the oven and allow to rest for ten minutes before slicing.

The lamb goes well with Goat Cheese and Potato Custard (recipe on page 135). Unmold the custard cups and place on a serving plate. Ladle one-and-a-half ounces of the sauce in front of the custard. Slice and arrange half a lamb loin on each plate. Garnish as desired and serve.

Scott Bemis, President

Denver Business Journal

Lorain, Ohio, a steel town of 75,000, is where Scott Bemis began his life journey. The president of the Denver Business Journal says: "This is the fourth market I have had the privilege to work in. It doesn't get any better than this."

Walking through the quiet atmosphere of the Journal offices, one would hardly suspect this is a place with hectic deadlines. How does he manage? Scott says, "Our staff members know that it's my mission to make this the best job they have ever had." Yes, the forty members are expected to work hard, but knowing there is someone who leads by example and is accessible ninety percent of the time helps to take the sting out.

ham loaf

Scott Bemis, Denver Business Journal, 2004 chairman of the Denver Metro Convention & Visitors Bureau

Serves six, approximately. This is absolutely the best ham loaf! It has that sweet flavor that comes from the brown sugar and ground ham combination.

1-1/2 pounds ground ham

1 pound ground pork

1 cup milk

1 cup cracker crumbs

1-1/2 cups brown sugar

2/3 cup vinegar

1/3 cup water

1-1/2 teaspoons dry mustard

1/2 cup prepared mustard

1/2 cup mayonnaise

Combine the ground ham with the pork. Add the milk and cracker crumbs and blend well with a wooden spoon or your hands.

Spray a loaf pan with Pam; pat the mixture into a loaf in the pan.

In a saucepan combine the brown sugar, vinegar, water and dry mustard. Heat to dissolve the sugar and pour over the ham loaf. Bake at 350-degrees for one-and-a-half hours, basting with the ham sauce.

Combine the prepared mustard and mayonnaise to serve with the loaf.

ÿ *Scott Bemis* ÿ

Terry Burns, Photographer

Terry Burns Photography

Traveling three-to-four days a week and making a good living out of it sounds like a good deal, right? But for this "chef" it was anything but. As a sales manager for Oracle Corporation, Terry Burns knew he had to make a change.

Because he was intrigued with photography, Terry decided to study under distinguished photographer Jim Hanson. Today, Terry Burns has his own business that offers a full range of photographic services with a personal touch and creative flair. He definitely enjoys photographing good food…and sharing his tantalizing creations with friends.

Terry is also someone who has searched for inner truths and a way to help others. As a member of the Mankind Project, a nonprofit organization of men working together to improve their lives and help other men, he even enjoys traveling again.

ÿ **Terry Burns** ÿ

baked steak

Terry Burns, Terry Burns Photography

Serves three to four. This recipe was described as easy to put together and delicious. Our recipe testers were asked to be "brutally honest," so you can trust the description.

2 tablespoons ground coffee

2 tablespoons grillmate's steak seasoning

one round or flank steak, approximately 1-1/2" thick

2 cups flour, divided

olive oil

2 cans cooked tomatoes

1 stalk celery, chopped

1 large sliced onion

8-10 sliced mushrooms

1 cup water

1 sliced red pepper

1 sliced green pepper

Mix ground coffee and steak seasoning. Spread mixture across both sides of steak. Dredge both sides of steak in flour.

Brown the steak in heated olive oil over medium heat, approximately two minutes per side. Transfer to a baking pan with a lid or to a cooking bag in an open pan.

Combine the tomatoes, celery, onion and mushrooms in a large mixing bowl. Add water and flour as necessary to keep a fluid but thick mixture. Pour mixture over the steak. Cover the baking pan or seal the cooking bag and bake for two to two-and-a-quarter hours at 350 degrees.

After the first hour, add the red and green peppers.

"Cooking is a way to not only create fun, but to create something while connecting with those I find enjoyable."
—Terry Burns

firehouse pork chops

Roland Seno, Littleton Fire Department

Serves six. Roland says, "This recipe is popular in the firehouse."

4 granny smith apples

6 pork chops

1 cup apple juice

2 cups brown sugar

3 teaspoons ground cloves

4 teaspoons cinnamon

1 teaspoon ground nutmeg

1 teaspoon ground allspice

1 cup raisins

Pre-heat oven to 325 degrees; pour apple juice into a 9" x 11" baking dish. Place the pork chops in the dish. Cut the apples into eighths.

Combine the brown sugar, cloves, nutmeg, cinnamon and allspice together in a brown-paper lunch bag. Twist top of the bag and shake to mix ingredients. Add a handful of apple slices to the bag and shake to coat. Place the apples on top of the pork chops. Continue until all the apples are coated and on the pork chops. Pour the remaining brown sugar mix over the chops. Top with raisins; bake covered at 325 degrees for forty-five minutes. Then cook another fifteen minutes uncovered. Serve and enjoy!

ÿ **Roland Seno** ÿ

When asked when he started cooking, Roland Seno stopped, thought and responded, "I don't remember a time when I did not cook." As one of three children, young Roland learned his culinary secrets watching his father on weekends. The cooking would start early on Sundays; the aromatic sauce would simmer until mid-afternoon when the family gathered for a meal. As a recipe that has passed from one generation to the next, the Sunday Sauce is a memorable Italian dish.

At age eighteen, Roland became the youngest fire fighter to be hired in Colorado. Many accolades followed over the next thirty years. Roland has even delivered three babies. Three! Today, as Operations Chief, he oversees all Littleton fire stations, a position that keeps him hopping.

Roland is more than an occasional cook. "There are cooks and then there are chefs," he says. "Cooks simply throw things together, but a chef has passion for what he cooks and goes the extra mile to get good ingredients."

The desire to cook, as we have seen from so many of the other *Denver Men in the Kitchen*, comes from the love of good food and the preparation of it, but more often than not, there's family tradition in the mix as well.

grandma rosie's sunday sauce

Roland J. Seno, Littleton Fire Department

Even if you are having meatballs with this, still add the Italian sausage to the sauce.

See page 77 for the meatball recipe.

Roland recalls, "Sunday Sauce can be made anytime, but frequently was made on Sundays when I was growing up. I have fond memories of this sauce being started early on a Sunday morning before we went to church and then simmering all day. It was always fun for me and my brother and sister to dip Italian bread in the sauce throughout the day to test it. This recipe was passed down from my paternal grandmother, Rosie Seno."

1/8 cup of olive oil

1-1/2 pounds of italian sausage

1 medium white onion, diced

6 cloves of garlic, diced small

6 twenty-eight ounce cans of whole peeled tomatoes

to taste ground black pepper

10 basil leaves

to taste italian seasoning

pasta

grated romano cheese

Using a large sauce pan on medium heat, brown the one-inch pieces of sausage in oil for five minutes. Add diced garlic and onion to pan. Lower heat and stir occasionally. Do not burn garlic or onion.

Process tomatoes in a blender for five-to-ten seconds; then add to the pan, making sure heat is low.

Add one teaspoon ground black pepper, basil leaves torn into four pieces each, and one tablespoon of Italian seasoning or to taste. Stir and cook covered for five hours over a low heat, stirring every fifteen-to-twenty minutes.

Remove the lid; cook uncovered while continuing to stir occasionally for another hour. Serve over your favorite pasta, topped with grated Romano cheese.

grandpa seno's meatballs

Roland Seno, Littleton Fire Department

Serves six to eight. This is a recipe Roland's father, Richard Seno, passed down to him.

1 pound 90% lean ground beef

1 pound 80% lean ground beef

2 heaping tablespoons grated romano cheese

2 large eggs

5 small cloves of garlic

1 cup italian bread crumbs

1/4 cup chopped fresh parsley, leaves only

1 level tablespoon salt

to taste ground pepper

olive oil

Mix all ingredients except oil together well. Make two-inch meatballs.

Heat olive oil in medium heat in a frying pan. Cook meatballs on two sides only, to a deep brown color.

Put meatballs and olive oil into pasta sauce two hours prior to serving. Skim off oil and serve.

Jeff Carr, Vineyard Entrepreneur

Garfield Estates Vineyard and Winery

After working eighteen years in the technical industry, Jeff Carr decided a change was in the wind. He and his former co-worker, Dave McLoughlin, along with their wives, Carol and Jan, purchased a farm in Palisade, Colorado, from the granddaughter of the family that originally homesteaded the land more than a century ago.

Starting his vineyard, Garfield Estates, from scratch, Jeff now has five varieties of wines, two of which have won major awards at the Annual Colorado Mountain Winefest. When you experience their tasting room, you are encouraged to take your time, sip the wines—and spend time with the owners, Jeff and Dave. He says, "Making great wine is part of it, but creating a place where people can spend two hours talking to the owners is just as much a part of the dream."

Jeff says his horizons broadened to include cooking after marriage. "It is the influence of my wife that gave me the impetus to learn how to cook. I did not come from a family where the men cooked, but I do enjoy creating something in the kitchen."

boeuf bourguignonne

Jeff Carr, Garfield Estates Vineyard and Winery

This is a terrific red-wine beef stew that makes six-to-eight servings.

1 bay leaf

12 peppercorns

1 teaspoon allspice

1/2 teaspoon thyme

1 teaspoon oregano

1/2 teaspoon rosemary

1-1/4 to 2 pounds boneless beef stew meat, cubed

olive oil

1 white onion, sliced or diced

1 cup thick-sliced carrots

6 red potatoes, cut in half

1/2 cup diced celery, including tops

2 cloves of garlic, smashed and diced

1 cup mushrooms, sliced thick

1 fourteen-ounce can stewed tomatoes

1 cup garfield estates syrah

2 cups beef stock or broth

to taste salt

2 tablespoons flour

1 tablespoon butter

Tie the bay leaf, allspice, thyme, oregano, rosemary, and peppercorns into a cheesecloth spice bag. Dredge meat in one tablespoon of flour and brown in a frying pan with a light film of olive oil. Brown meat on all sides and transfer the meat to a stew pot/casserole dish.

Turn the onion, carrots, garlic, celery and red potatoes into the frying pan, adding fresh oil if necessary. Brown the vegetables lightly before transferring them over the beef.

Pour the can of tomatoes into the frying pan, breaking up the whole tomatoes and scraping up juices. Pour into stew pot.

Add the red wine, beef stock, the spice bag and salt. Stew the beef on top of stove for two-and-a-half hours, turning and basting the meat several times. Add the mushrooms for the last forty-five minutes of cooking time.

Remove spice bag and discard. Finally, to thicken the stew, mash one tablespoon flour and one tablespoon butter into a thick paste; stir in to thicken, and serve.

ỹ Jeff Carr ỹ

Michael (Mick) Angelo Rosacci, Chef & Author

Tony's Meats & Specialty Foods

For many of us, Saturday morning wouldn't be the same without Chef Mick and his cooking lessons on Channel 7. There he can be found whipping up down-to-earth and delicious concoctions that even the most inexperienced cooks can follow. Look for his culinary columns in the local newspapers, too.

Mick's father, Tony Rosacci, came to Colorado in 1971, seeking a better life for his family. But as the top executive of a grocery chain, he decided that his busy life style was not conducive to bringing up his family. In 1978 he opened Tony's Meats and Mick followed in his footsteps.

Because he's on the road often, Mick says he's extended his study to cuisines of other countries. Being a single dad with two sons has been good background for him to create wholesome meals they'll eat. A bit of a pioneer, this chef-TV personality was preparing ready-to-cook meals at Tony's Meat Market ten years before it was fashionable.

Mick's father always said to him, "You measure success by the number of people at your table at the Christmas meal."

Mick Rosacci

osso buco with pine nut gremolata

Michael (Chef Mick) Rosacci, Tony's Meats & Specialty Foods

Serves six. This recipe got a top rating from our testers.

4 pounds veal shanks, cut 1 1/2" thick

olive oil

salt and pepper

flour

1 small onion, minced

1 carrot, minced

1 stalk celery, minced

2 cloves garlic, crushed

1 fourteen-ounce can italian tomatoes with juice, diced

2 cups dry white wine

2 cups chicken stock

2-3 sprigs fresh thyme

1 bay leaf

gremolata:

1/4 cup chopped italian parsley

1/4 cup toasted pine nuts

zest of one lemon

Season veal shanks with salt and pepper, then dredge in flour. Heat a heavy sauté pan or Dutch oven and add two tablespoons oil. Brown shanks in batches, adding more oil as needed. Remove and reserve shanks.

Add onion, carrots, celery, garlic and pinches of salt to pan, cooking and stirring until tender and starting to brown. Stir in tomatoes, wine, stock and herbs and then browned veal shanks; bring to a boil. Reduce heat to a simmer and cover tightly. Simmer slowly or roast in a 325-degree oven for about two hours or until veal is tender and almost falling off the bone. Meanwhile, combine Gremolata ingredients and set aside.

Remove shanks to a platter and skim fat. Taste and adjust sauce as desired: boiling to reduce, adjusting seasoning, or thickening with Wondra superfine flour. Serve shanks and sauce with Risotto Milanese, creamy polenta or mashed potatoes, sprinkling with Gremolata to taste.

David Avrin,
Public Relations Specialist

Avrin Public Relations

A decade ago, David Avrin was handling PR for Children's Hospital by day and performing in an a "cappella" group called the Diners by night, opening for some of the greats like Ray Charles. Today he is a self-described "boring suburban dad." Settling down means David tries to leave work by 5:00 p.m. to spend evenings with his wife and three kids, enjoying his "Daddy time." He says he came to realize that, "Deep inside, I was always a backyard-barbecuing, sports coaching, Cub Scouts, suburban kind of dad, and that has always been my dream."

As president of the Avrin Public Relations Group, David Avrin, PR specialist, spends his spare time creating awareness for products, companies and persona, from best-selling authors and sports celebrities to business leaders and other entrepreneurs. He also has developed a strong reputation for generating positive news media coverage for his clients.

ℽ *David Avrin* ℽ

zippy pepper-jack breakfast casserole

David Avrin, Avrin Public Relations

This is a great buffet dish.

1/4 cup melted butter

1 twenty-four ounce package frozen
shredded hash browns

1 brick shredded pepper jack cheese

3 thin slices of cooked ham, diced

1 cup of sliced mushrooms

2 cups milk

14–18 eggs

1/4 teaspoon salt

Sprinkle the entire bag of hash browns into large greased casserole dish. Bake hash browns at 425 degrees for thirty-to-forty minutes until they begin to look toasted.

Sprinkle cheese, mushrooms and ham evenly over entire surface.

Beat eggs and milk in a large bowl; add salt and mix well. Pour the entire mixture over the top of the other ingredients. Bake uncovered for forty-five to fifty-five minutes until browned and a knife inserted in the center comes out clean.

brown veal sauce

Mark Black, Executive Chef, Brown Palace Hotel

Yields a half gallon. One pound of mirepoix is equal parts of onion, celery and carrots that add up to one pound of vegetables.

1 pound mirepoix

4 ounces clarified butter

4 ounces all purpose flour

3 quarts brown veal stock, (see note)

4 ounces tomato puree

1 sachet (see lamb stock recipe for sachet ingredients)

salt and pepper to taste

In a saucepot, sauté the mirepoix in butter until browned. Add the flour and stir continually until you have a brown roux.

Add the stock and tomato puree. Stir until all the roux is broken up. Bring to a boil, then reduce the heat until it simmers. Add the sachet. Simmer for one hour.

Strain the sauce through a strainer lined with layers of cheesecloth.

Season with salt and pepper and either cool down or hold hot until needed.

Note: Use the lamb stock recipe conversion, page 85, for the veal stock recipe.

lamb stock

Mark Black, Executive Chef, Brown Palace Hotel

Yields one gallon. For a veal stock, simply substitute veal bones for the lamb bones. The mirepoix is equal parts chopped onion, carrots and celery.

1 bay leaf

1 teaspoon dried thyme

1/2 teaspoon crushed peppercorns

2 cloves crushed garlic

5 pounds lamb bones

2 gallons cold water

1 pound mirepoix

4 ounces tomato paste

For the sachet: Wrap the bay leaf, dried thyme, peppercorns, cloves and garlic in cheesecloth and tie with a string.

Put the bones in a single layer in a roasting pan; brown bones in the oven at 375 degrees. Turn occasionally to brown evenly.

Remove bones and put them in a stockpot. Pour off the fat from the roasting pan and reserve.

Deglaze roasting pan on the stove with some of the cold water. Add the liquid from the roasting pan to the stockpot. Add remaining water until the bones are covered. Bring to a boil, then reduce heat to a simmer.

Spoon some of the fat reserved into the roasting pan and sauté the mirepoix until browned. Add the tomato paste and mix completely with the mirepoix. Add to the stockpot, along with the sachet, and continue to simmer for four-to-five hours. Strain the stock and cool.

Eugene Dilbeck, Partner

Lambert-Dilbeck Marketing Resources

Hospitality begins in the home—and Eugene and Lynette Dilbeck's home has the feel of elegant comfort that is afforded in a casual dining atmosphere. Coming from a rural setting has lent Eugene that likeable quality of "country." It is no wonder his favorite dishes are beef and wild game. Though he is an entrepreneur at heart, he also finds enjoyment in the traditional activities, such as tending garden and cooking at home for friends and family.

Eugene has also restored a '55 Chevy that looks as new as the day it was driven off the assembly line—complete with original hub cabs. "It is the one-hundred percent authentic cars that are the most valuable," he says.

❦ Eugene Dilbeck ❦

dilbeck's denver ribs

Eugene Dilbeck, Lambert-Dilbeck Marketing Resources

Simple and easy to do for that beginner. Use your favorite barbecue sauce or try what the Dilbecks prefer, Hammett's Mild Sauce.

2 or 3 meaty beef ribs per person

your favorite barbecue sauce

Wash and dry the ribs; set them side-by-side on top of broiler pan with water in bottom and cover lightly with aluminum foil. Use two pans if necessary, but stacking the ribs is not recommended.

Bake the ribs at 175-to-200 degrees for approximately six-to-ten hours, depending upon the amount of ribs. Also check periodically to make sure that there is enough water in the bottom to continue steaming. (Best guess is eight-to-ten hours for eight-to-ten ribs). Ribs should be gray/brown and starting to pull away from the bone. A lot of the rib meat will actually fall off the bone when lifted.

Carefully remove ribs from oven. Dip each rib individually in bowl of barbecue sauce.

Preheat grill to medium high. Grill ribs five-to-ten minutes, basting often, until each is glazed. Serve messy ribs with warm sauce, napkins and toothpicks.

Mike Jenson, Graphic Designer

Jenson Advertising

Here is a guy who cannot make it in the kitchen; he creates his cuisine over the open flame. As a Boy Scout he learned his culinary secrets as Scout Master for ten years. He cooks on everything from gas to charcoal, to open flames or a smoker depending upon the dish desired. He states, "When you're camping, anything tastes good. If you drop it in the dirt, it becomes mountain seasoning."

One year, he even cooked a Thanksgiving dinner over a makeshift oven just to prove it could be done; it came complete with the pumpkin pie. This holiday treat was served in the wild at ten below on a tablecloth-covered table. Amazing.

Michael's love for creating the different and unusual is seen in his business with his friendly smile and outstretched hand to his clients. He is even still working with the very first client he took on in 1972 when he opened Jenson Advertising. The secret of his success can be seen in his willingness to help others, with ten percent of his creations going as pro bono to non-profit groups. What goes around certainly comes around and for this awesome graphic artist, the success is evidence enough.

beef tenderloin stuffed with garlic

Mike Jenson, Jenson Advertising

Mike says the recipe is also great with a peppercorn sauce. He also prefers McCormick's steak seasoning.

1 beef tenderloin, 4-5 pounds

6-8 cloves of garlic, cut in half

steak seasoning

Prepare charcoal in a covered grill. Trim excess fat from tenderloin. With a sharp knife make slits about one-inch deep randomly in the meat and insert a half of a garlic clove in each slit. The slit may be deeper if needed.

Rub the tenderloin lightly with steak seasoning. Tie with cooking string.

Place stuffed tenderloin on the grill and sear on all sides, turning frequently, for about fifteen-to-twenty minutes. Move the charcoal to form a circle. Place the meat above the center of the circle on the grill.

Cover grill, open vents halfway. Cook until an instant meat thermometer inserted into the meat registers 135 degrees for medium-rare or 145 degrees for medium.

When done, place tenderloin on a warmed platter, cover loosely with aluminum foil and let rest for ten minutes. Carve across the grain into three-quarter-inch to one-inch slices.

Serves four-to-six beef lovers.

ÿ *Mike Jenson* ÿ

luscious
soups, sauces & drinks

red chili • steve's green chili • fresh strawberries with champagne sabayon • tom's chili • steve's tomato salsa • manhattan fish chowder • teriyaki chicken marinade • chilled watermelon soup with honeydew "ice" • sparkling strawberry mint lemonade • easy egg drop soup • maple steak marinade • thai chicken marinade for grilling • butternut squash soup • corn chowder • mushroom soup • clam chowder • black bean salsa • corn relish

red chili

Ron Henderson, Denver Film Society

Ron Henderson makes his red chili recipe for the International Film Festival Annual Staff Party—this is a twenty-five-year tradition. As a hearty chili recipe, this is a sure crowd-pleaser.

3 pounds ground chuck

2 large red onions, chopped

1 large red bell pepper

1 large green bell pepper

2 garlic cloves, minced

1 tablespoon oregano

2 tablespoons ground cumin

3-4 tablespoons chili powder

1 fourteen-ounce can tomato paste

to taste salt and pepper

to taste worcestershire sauce

tapati'o sauce to taste

2-3 jalapeño peppers, chopped

2 poblano peppers, chopped

2 chipotles, chopped

Brown the chuck in a large pot; drain the juice. Sauté the onion and green and red bell peppers. Add onions, bells, garlic, oregano, cumin and chili powder. Mix in the tomato paste.

Add one-quart hot water and bring to a boil.

Season to taste and add jalapeño, poblano and chipotle peppers; simmer for three hours, stirring often.

ꙮ Ron Henderson ꙮ

Intriguing and sophisticated are words that describe Ron Henderson, founder and artistic director of the Denver Film Society. "I live life at 24 frames per second. People who know film know what that means." By definition, that's fast.

From biking to tennis to traveling with his wife to cooking, Ron has one busy life style. But there is down time, he says, which usually includes another favorite pursuit: reading biographies about such greats as Catherine Hepburn, James Dean and Sylvia Plath.

As someone well-acquainted with the film culture, Ron wrote *The Imagemaker* in 1972, a book of interviews with film directors and a collection of essays on the film culture. Before starting the Denver Film Society, he was book editor at MacMillan, the director of the National Student Film Festival in New York City, the founder of the Breckenridge Festival of Film and the program director of the Taos, New Mexico, "Talking Picture Festival."

Steve Lutton, Owner

Renegade Press

From the soil to the table…every spring Steve Lutton starts early preparing his soil and planting seeds. Summers are for cultivating; in the fall, he spends time preserving his garden for cold winter nights. He takes pride in knowing that the results of his tender gardening will eventually be served to his family and friends. One taste of his pure products convinces you that his efforts are well worth it.

Steve is part owner of Renegade Press and has a finance degree from Ohio State University. He learned gardening while working at a nursery during summer breaks from college. His culinary interests were piqued while working at an Italian restaurant supply house during that time.

Steve says he's in Colorado because of the mountains. Thinking that he would just visit Colorado on a ski trip in 1985, Steve fell in love with the Colorado terrain. As someone who loves skiing during winter months, he does manage to steal away for a whirl down the mountain. In summer, he and Cheri have been known to run a half-marathon or two.

ở *Steve Lutton* ở

steve's green chili

Steven H. Lutton, Renegade Press

Yields approximately twenty cups. This recipe serves a crowd. It also is great as a do-ahead for those south-of-the-border recipes that call for green chili.

25-30 large green chilies

6 pounds pork ribs or shoulder

3 tablespoons fresh sage leaves

15 cloves garlic, peeled

3 tablespoons olive oil

6 large (half-ripe) tomatoes

3 large yellow onions

10-20 jalapeño peppers

1 tablespoon salt

1/2 teaspoon ground white pepper

1 tablespoon ground cumin

sour cream and shredded cheese

Roast green chilies on a hot gas grill, peel and seed. You can also use three large cans of green chilies instead of the fresh.

Separate pork meat from bone and cut into half-inch cubes.

Mince sage leaves and garlic. Combine with pork. Heat olive oil in large skillet, brown pork on all sides. (Do not cook through the pork.)

Put browned pork mixture into large stockpot and add one cup of water.

Chop tomatoes, onions and chilies. Remove seeds from jalapeños and finely chop. Use twenty for a hot batch, ten for a medium batch. Add to the pork.

Bring to a simmer, adding salt and white pepper. Continue simmering the chili, stirring occasionally for one hour. Stir in the cumin. Simmer and stir occasionally for an additional three hours. Top with sour cream and shredded cheddar.

tom's chili

Tom Green, KWGN-TV, WB2

The chocolate gives this chili a unique flavor.

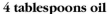

4 tablespoons oil

2 onions, diced

2 garlic cloves, minced

2 tablespoons chili powder

3 two-pound cans drained italian tomatoes (5-6 cups)

2 cups water

2 squares unsweetened chocolate

4 tablespoons sugar

1 tablespoon salt

2 pounds beef, round or chuck, cut into 1/2" cubes

1 or 2 cans drained kidney beans, 2-4 cups

Cook onions and garlic in hot oil until lightly browned. Add chili powder, cook over medium heat, stirring for two-to-three minutes. Add tomatoes and water. Lower heat and simmer for five minutes. Add chocolate, sugar and salt, stirring until chocolate is melted. Simmer, covered, for one hour.

Cook beef in hot oil, until lightly browned. Add meat to sauce and simmer for two more hours, covered.

Add beans and heat through. Cool. Cover and refrigerate. Degrease, reheat and serve the following day.

Interesting...in doing research for this book, we've found that some of the guys who cook occasionally, what they do create is terrific. Tom Green is one of them.

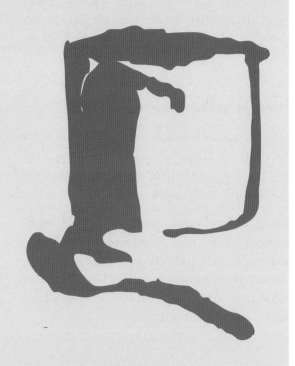

Tom Green, Announcer

KWGN-TV WB2

From his friendly smile to his easy manner, Tom Green welcomes each day as anchorman for WB2 Morning News. The single father of a son, Tom says, "I don't cook that often, but there are times it is a necessity."

Tom grew up in New York and attended Ithaca College. His tenure in the Denver market is marked by ten Emmy awards and being named the Colorado Sportscaster of the Year four times by National Sportscasters and Sportswriters Associations. Previously Tom was sports anchor for more than thirteen years for KUSA-TV (NBC) in Denver after working for ESPN.

ÿ **Tom Green** ÿ

fresh strawberries with champagne sabayon

Nicholas C. Moschetti, Chef and Manager, Bisetti's Ristorante

Serves three to four. For best results, make sure the strawberries are fresh, clean and ripe. The results depend upon it.

1/2 pound strawberries, cleaned and quartered

1 cup sugar, divided

6 egg yolks

1-1/2 cups dry champagne

1/2 teaspoon vanilla extract

Toss the cleaned strawberries in one-quarter cup of the sugar and place in the refrigerator.

To make the Sabayon sauce: In a medium stainless steel bowl combine the egg yolks and remaining sugar; whip until light and fluffy. Add the champagne and the vanilla extract. Cook over a pot of boiling water, whisk continuously to keep the eggs from curdling until the mixture is thick and hot. The sauce should be thick and fluffy at this point.

Pour over the strawberries and serve immediately.

strawberries

strawberries

strawberries

steve's tomato salsa

Steven H. Lutton, Renegade Press

This is a perfect flavor for topping Steve's Huevos Rancheros, page 41.

10-12 pounds fresh ripe tomatoes

1 small white onion

12 cloves garlic

1 small bunch green onions

6 jalapeño peppers

1/2 cup diced roasted green chilies

1 cup vinegar

4 tablespoons lime juice

1 tablespoon salt

Prepare tomatoes by plunging into boiling water until they split, then into cold water. Peel, quarter and remove sloppy pulp and seeds. Cut into large chunks. Measure into a large stockpot to yield fifteen cups.

Mince white onion and garlic. Slice green onions, both white and green parts. Combine everything and bring to a simmer for ten minutes.

Yields ten-to-twelve pints. If canning, use standard hot water process. Refrigerate for immediate use.

tomatos

tomatos

tomatos

Ÿ Jim Saxton Ÿ

manhattan fish chowder

James Saxton, Excel Services Network, Inc.

Yield 8 servings. The recipe calls for pollock fish, but you may substitute blue fish, striped bass, trout or catfish for the pollock. In Colorado the pollock may have to be ordered.

8-10 whole plum tomatoes

1 pound boneless pollock

1/4 cup olive oil

3 medium garlic cloves, peeled and crushed

1 cup onion, finely diced

1/2 cup celery, finely diced

1/4 teaspoon basil

1/4 teaspoon oregano

pinch thyme

1 cup tomato sauce

6 cups clam juice

3 teaspoons fresh parsley, chopped

salt to taste

Peel, seed and chop tomatoes into quarter-inch pieces or substitute two cups stewed tomatoes, finely chopped, without the juice. Cut the pollock into one-inch cubes.

In a four-quart soup pot, heat olive oil. Add garlic. When the garlic turns brown remove it quickly with a slotted spoon and discard. Reduce the heat. Add celery, onions and spices to oil. Cook over medium heat for five minutes.

Add tomatoes and tomato sauce; simmer for five minutes. Add clam juice and pollock. Cover and bring to a boil.

Remove cover and boil for ten minutes longer. With a wire whisk, whip soup to break up fish into pea-sized flakes. Reduce to simmer and cook for twenty minutes.

Add parsley and salt to taste. You may also serve by ladling soup over rice primavera in a soup crock.

Jim Saxton, President

Excel Services Network, Inc.

Jim Saxton lives by the old adage: "If you want to be successful, do what everyone else doesn't want to do and do it better then anyone else." Jim cleans houses—and does it very well. On a daily basis, he handles the operations of three offices that send out about thirty crews per day for a lot of appreciative people. He makes life easier for his clients.

Jim has had other, more lucrative business opportunities, he says, but turned them down. As a small business owner: "I have the ability to be with daughter Emily when she needs me. I can carve out time to be the father she needs." Cooking came as a necessity for this single dad. He'd had little experience until college, when he was faced with the choice of learning how to cook or eating pizza every night.

sparkling strawberry mint lemonade

Ian Kleinman, Executive Chef, Indigo Restaurant

Serves several. This is a delightful beverage, it's great for cooling the afternoon or for serving at a party.

1 cup water

2 cups sugar, divided

1-1/4 pints strawberries

1/4 cup mint leaves

2 cups fresh lemon juice

1 quart chilled sparkling water

In a small saucepan bring the water and one cup of sugar to a simmer, stirring until sugar is dissolved. Cool to room temperature.

Coarsely chop the strawberries. In a blender puree berries with the syrup, mint, lemon juice and remaining cup of sugar.

Pour puree through a sieve into a three-quart pitcher.

Just before serving mix in sparkling water.

Serve over ice and garnish with a lemon wedge.

Ian Kleinman, Executive Chef
Indigo Restaurant

Long hours are spent over hot stoves at Indigo. And Ian Kleinman's one-hundred percent effort pays off daily. "When people go out to celebrate birthdays, anniversaries, and holidays," he says, "restaurants are places where memories are made."

Ian and father Stephen Kleinman are talented executive chefs in their own right, but as a father and son team, they were the culinary duo asked to the prestigious James Beard house twice to collaborate on meal preparation. The first time was on Norwegian Independence Day 2001 and the second, Father's Day 2002. Since they are of Norwegian descent, these were timely occasions. The James Beard house is owned and operated by Julia Child; to be invited there is one of the highest honors a chef can receive.

ẏ *Ian Kleinman* ẏ

Chris Grosz, Police Officer
with the Community Outreach Unit

Littleton Police Department

Though this gentleman is an amateur "chef," he keeps up with the best of them, winning a first place in the miscellaneous category in the Frisco Challenge in 2001 for a Hickory Smoked Pork Loin. Taking his culinary pursuits to heart, Chris owns five grills and tackles everything from steaks to smoking turkeys.

Chris says he learned a lot of his cooking skills from his parents but his recipes are trial and error. Although he will share most recipes with friends, the recipe for his "rub" that he enters in competitions is so top secret that even book authors cannot weasel it out of him.

"In Community Outreach, I get a chance to do what most policemen don't," Chris says. "When I start a case, I see it through to the end. We do a lot in the community where we connect with citizens. I would like to thank my families, the one I was born into, the one I married into, and the one I work with. Especially my parents for giving me their interest and my wife for putting up with the errors." Friends, relatives, all who meet this "chef" feel welcomed by his friendly charm.

ÿ *Chris Grosz* ÿ

easy egg drop soup

Christopher S. Grosz, Littleton Police Department

Serves four. This is a recipe that is great after a hard day at the office when a quick meal is needed. Chris often works late at night and can be found in the kitchen, winding down, cooking this soup.

5 fourteen ounce cans chicken broth

1 carrot, peeled

5 scallions, just the greens

6 eggs

salt to taste

pepper to taste

soy sauce, optional

Place the cans of chicken broth in a large soup pot. Bring to a boil. While waiting for the boil, take the peeled carrot and peel off thin slices of the carrot; set that aside. Clean the scallions and dice into small pieces. When the broth is boiling, add the carrot slices and scallion pieces. Mix. Crack the six eggs into a small mixing bowl. Whip well.

After the broth has had a chance to boil and soften the carrots and onions, add the whipped eggs to the boiling mixture. Mix and remove from the heat. Add salt and pepper to taste while stirring occasionally. This may also be served with soy sauce.

maple steak marinade

Christopher S. Grosz, Littleton Police Department

Serves four. Chris has taken this recipe to competitions and won against even the professional chefs. You won't be sorry for choosing this recipe to marinate your favorite steaks.

4 large steaks, your favorite cut

4 bottles bass ale

2 cups maple syrup

4 teaspoons red pepper flakes

2 tablespoons greek seasoning

Pour the ale into a saucepan and heat to a simmer on medium heat. Simmer until reduced by half. Add the syrup, red pepper flakes and the seasoning. Mix and let cool. Marinate steaks overnight, turning them at least once.

The next day, remove steaks from the marinade. Rub with your favorite steak spice and grill over direct heat until desired doneness.

thai boneless chicken marinade for grilling

Bradley S. Freedberg, Attorney at Law

This is a sure crowd-pleaser; serves several. Try this during a Sunday afternoon football game. See page 174 for information on Brad Freedberg.

1 large pack chicken breasts

2 tablespoons olive oil

2 tablespoons thai chile paste

1 tablespoon yellow mustard

1 teaspoon brown sugar

1/2 teaspoon garlic powder

1/2 teaspoon white pepper

1 cup rice wine vinegar

Rinse the chicken. In casserole, mix the olive oil, Thai Chile Paste, yellow mustard, brown sugar, garlic powder, white pepper and rice wine vinegar.

Place chicken breasts in mixed marinade. Let marinate for two hours, turning once.

Grill chicken on outdoor grill until done, about five-to-ten minutes on both sides, depending on thickness of the chicken.

Ÿ Todd Friedman Ÿ

butternut squash soup

Todd Friedman, Chef, Women's Bean Project

Todd uses Myers rum for this recipe. Todd's Tips: "When cooking, fresh herbs are the best way to go." Use parsley, marjoram, oregano, savory, sage, thyme, basil and rosemary for the sachet. Some of the herbs are stronger than others, use according to strength. For instance, rosemary has a much stronger scent than marjoram, so use the rosemary in a smaller ratio. Chop all of your herbs finely. If you have extra, use it in all of your cooking.

1 butternut squash

1/2 onion diced

1 carrot diced

1 celery stalk diced

1 tablespoon chopped garlic

3 ounces oil

1/2 stick butter

kosher salt

cracked pepper

4 ounces dark rum

2 ounces white wine

32 ounces chicken or vegetable stock

1 banana

2 bay leaves

3 thyme sprigs

4 ounces heavy cream

fresh herbs

Peel, seed and cube the butternut squash. In a hot pan, sauté onions, garlic, carrots and celery with half the oil and one-quarter stick of butter; season with salt and pepper. When the onions are translucent, add the butternut squash, rest of oil and butter; season again with salt and pepper. Flambé with the rum, wait until flames die down, and then add the wine.

After the alcohol evaporates, add the stock, banana, bay leaf, and thyme sprigs. Bring soup to a boil, then let simmer for one-half hour or until squash is soft. Purée the soup with a hand blender or food processor, bring soup back to a boil with cream, simmer and adjust seasoning. Add fresh herbs and serve.

The Women's Bean Project is a non-profit business dedicated to helping women break the cycle of poverty and unemployment. Its goal is to provide each program participant with a safe, accepting work environment where she can learn to identify and build upon her talents while building the skills necessary to get and keep mainstream employment.

Todd Friedman, Chef

Women's Bean Project

This Denver Man in the Kitchen grew up in Queens, New York, and spent a year in a Kibbutz in Israel at age eighteen. There he worked in an optical factory, helped in the kitchen and in the fields.

In 1987 Todd changed direction, coming to Denver where his love for the culinary arts blossomed. Todd is now chef for the Women's Bean Project. He also works with PS1 Charter School preparing lunches, which includes teaching students and women from the Women's Bean Project in the culinary arts. Todd is now working toward a teaching degree at Metro State College.

As a diabetic, Todd knows firsthand the value of good nutrition; he regularly volunteers with diabetic kids. One's obstacles can sometimes be the greatest assets in helping others overcome their problems.

corn chowder

Todd Friedman, Chef, Women's Bean Project

Todd always uses fresh herbs as a way to show his guests he really cares. Use a sprinkling of parsley, marjoram, oregano, savory, sage, thyme, basil and rosemary.

6 cobs of corn	Cut the niblets of corn off the cobs.
4 ounces oil	In a hot pan add two ounces of oil and a fourth of a stick of butter. Add the onions, carrots, garlic and celery, with salt and pepper to taste. Sauté until onions are translucent.
1/2 stick butter	
1/2 onion, chopped	
1 carrot, chopped	Add the rest of the oil, butter, corn and potato; again salt and pepper to taste. Sauté for five-to-seven minutes, until all the vegetables are well-coated.
1 celery stalk, chopped	
1 large potato, cubed	
1 tablespoon garlic, chopped	Deglaze with the vermouth and wait until liquid has been evaporated.
6 ounces sweet vermouth	
3 ounces flour	Add the flour and mix into the ingredients; be careful not to burn the flour. This is easy to do.
24 ounces chicken or vegetable stock	Add the stock, bay leaves, and thyme sprigs; season with salt and pepper.
kosher salt	
cracked pepper	Simmer for about twenty-five minutes or until potatoes are soft. Purée with a hand blender or food processor. Be sure to take out bay leaf and thyme sprig. Add the cream, adjust the seasonings and bring back to a boil. Simmer for five minutes; add the herbs and serve.
3 bay leaves	
3 thyme sprigs	
6 ounces heavy cream	
fresh herbs	

mushroom soup

Todd Friedman, Chef, Women's Bean Project

Todd says, "The better the wine, the better the flavor."

1/2 onion, finely sliced

1 large carrot, finely sliced

1 stalk of celery, finely sliced

1 tablespoon finely chopped garlic

1/4 stick of butter

2 ounces of cooking oil

6 ounces of sherry wine

1-1/2 pounds of freshly sliced mushroom buttons

24 ounces of chicken stock or vegetable stock

bay leaf

3 sprigs of fresh thyme

6 ounces of heavy cream

kosher salt to taste

cracked pepper to taste

1/4 cup fresh herbs (such as parsley, marjoram, oregano, savory, sage, thyme, basil and rosemary)

In a hot pan, sauté onions, garlic, carrots and celery with one ounce of oil and half of the butter until onions are translucent; season with salt and pepper. Add the rest of the oil and butter with the mushrooms; mix the mushrooms until covered with oil and butter, season again with salt and pepper.

When the mushrooms have broken down and are soft, five-to-seven minutes, deglaze with the sherry. Let the liquid cook down until three-fourths of the liquid has evaporated. Add stock, bay leaf, thyme; bring to a boil, and adjust seasoning, salt and pepper. Let the soup simmer for about twenty minutes.

Using a hand blender is the quickest way to purée the soup, but a food processor or blender also will work. Be sure to take out the bay leaf and thyme. After the soup is puréed, add the heavy cream and bring back up to a boil. Simmer for five minutes; add the fresh herbs and serve.

I have served the soup without puréeing the mixture… Chef's choice.

clam chowder

By Michael Sagrillo, Chef and Owner, Bisetti's Ristorante

Serves six to eight. Michael says, "Sautéing dry herbs and spices will wake them up, giving the dish better flavor and aroma."

1 tablespoon canola oil

1/2 pound bacon

2 cups diced yellow onions

2 cups diced portabello mushrooms

1-1/2 cups diced carrots

2 cups diced celery

1/2 stick unsalted butter

1 teaspoon red pepper flakes

1 tablespoon minced fresh garlic

1 tablespoon kosher salt

1 tablespoon dried thyme

46 ounces clam juice

16 ounces chopped clams

3 cups diced red potatoes

2 cups whole corn kernels

1 pint heavy cream

2 tablespoons cornstarch

1/3 cup water

Slice bacon into strips one-quarter inch by one inch and sauté in oil.

Once the bacon fat is cooked out, add the onion, celery, carrots and mushrooms; sauté until the onions are translucent. Use the butter to add cooking fat midway through this process. Add the garlic and dry spices.

Slowly add the clam juice; as it hits the pot it will loosen the good flavors stuck to the bottom. Add chopped clams and simmer for one hour.

Add potatoes and continue to simmer until they are al dente, firm yet done.

Add corn and cream; bring to boil. Note, for extra flavor you may grill whole corn on the cob and then cut the kernels off.

Place the cornstarch and cool water in a bowl and mix, then add mixture to boiling chowder to thicken.

His love for good eats was the initial impetus for learning to cook.

Michael Sagrillo, Chef & Owner
Bisetti's Ristorante

Michael Sagrillo...now here is a guy who likes to grow what he eats; when not at work, Michael is at home with family and gardening. In fact, his hobbies, Mike says, are wine, kids, cooking, sports and gardening (and maybe not in that order).

His love for good eats was the initial impetus for learning to cook. Michael started as a dishwasher, working his way up at this popular restaurant to owner. He also graduated from Johnson & Wales Culinary School.

For Michael, being a connoisseur of good wine goes hand-in-hand with owning a restaurant like Bisetti's. Like a lot of passionate artists, his cooking is always evolving. He says, "Eating a meal is an experience. It is not just putting food in front of someone; it is the total experience from meal preparation to final delivery that makes the moment."

ϓ *Michael Sagrillo* ϓ

black bean salsa

Stephen S. Kleinman, Executive Chef, Colorado Convention Center

Serves six to eight. This is great as a go-together with the Szechuan Chicken Tacos, page 49, or simply as a side dish salsa.

1/2 pound dried black beans

1 medium yellow onion, halved

1 tablespoon ground cumin

1 bay leaf

1 pound roma tomatoes, diced

1 cup diced red onion

1 cup diced jicama

1/2 cup diced jalapeño pepper

1/2 cup diced green pepper

2 tablespoons chopped cilantro

2 teaspoons kosher salt

2 teaspoons lime juice

In a one-and-a-half quart pot, cover beans with water and cook with onion, cumin and bay leaf until soft, about one-and-a-half hours. Drain, discard onion and bay leaf, and let cool.

Combine the beans with remaining ingredients. Let stand at least thirty minutes before serving, or cover and refrigerate up to three days.

corn relish

Stephen Kleinman, Executive Chef, Colorado Convention Center

This is a great add-to-the-table item or in combination with the Szechuan Chicken Tacos.

6 ears sweet corn, husks on

1 green bell pepper, diced

1 red bell pepper, diced

1 small red onion, diced

1/4 cup cider vinegar

1 tablespoon each salt and pepper

Fold husks back, remove silk and fold husks back over the ears. Grill ears for about twenty minutes or until the husks are dark. Cool and remove kernels from corn.

In a one-and-a-half quart bowl, combine corn, peppers, onion, vinegar, salt and pepper.

Let stand at least thirty minutes before serving, or cover and refrigerate for up to three days.

corn relish

relish

relish

relish

relish

relish

corn

relish

relish

bell pepper

healthy & veggie

hickenlooper's healthy tofu spaghetti • broccoli salad • colorado corn packets • incredibly healthy hummus with fatoush • pommes berny • samfaina • butter mushrooms with port • artichokes al canzano • energy bars • portabello smoked gouda and red pepper panini • goat cheese & potato custard • linguini & artichokes • papa chinese • spicy grilled corn on the cob • spinach-cheese quiche • spinach, artichoke & asparagus salad • jicama citrus salad • stir-fried zucchini & yellow squash • fried spaghetti

Mayor John Hickenlooper

City and County of Denver

This mayor has brought new energy to Denver, creating a climate where the city partners with the business community and non-profit sector to generate opportunities for all. His regional approach to economic development, transit and the arts is building bridges to community throughout the region.

"I used to think running one of the most popular restaurants in Denver was the best job in the city, " Hickenlooper says, "but now I know it was only the second best. Being the mayor of the Mile High City is the greatest job!"

Mayor Hickenlooper learned how to cook in college and the geologist-turned-entrepreneur went on to open Colorado's first brewpub, the Wynkoop Brewing Company, in 1988. In addition to bringing customers to Lower Downtown, he helped bring residents as well by developing the Wynkoop Lofts, Mercantile Square and the Titanium Building. As the owner of six Denver neighborhood restaurants, we bet this mayor's recipes are top-notch.

ÿ *Mayor John Hickenlooper* ÿ

john hickenlooper's tofu spaghetti

John Hickenlooper, Mayor of Denver

Serves at least four. This recipe would also work well with chicken in place of tofu, for all you chicken lovers.

2 fourteen-ounce cans tomato sauce

1 can diced chopped tomatoes

2 teaspoons basil, divided

1/2 teaspoon sweet marjoram

1 teaspoon oregano

olive oil

1/2 pound tofu, chopped into 1/2" cubes

1 red onion diced

2 large cloves garlic, divided

1/2 pound fresh mushrooms, chopped into 1/2" pieces

red wine

your favorite spaghetti

In a cast-iron frying pan, combine the tomato sauce, chopped tomatoes, one teaspoon basil, marjoram, oregano and one teaspoon olive oil. Simmer for one hour.

Let tofu drain on paper towel for thirty minutes.

In another frying pan on medium high heat, add one tablespoon olive oil and the onions. Add one teaspoon basil, one clove minced garlic, and salt and pepper to taste. Just before the onion is brown, add mushrooms. Add more oil if needed.

In the same pan with all of the juices left in, add tofu, one tablespoon of oil, one large minced garlic clove, basil, salt and pepper. Saute on medium high until it is brown.

Pour the tomato sauce into the pan with the tofu and onions and simmer one-half hour. Add one-fourth cup of red wine if sauce is too thick. Add mushroom mixture just prior to serving over spaghetti.

broccoli salad

Roland J. Seno, Littleton Fire Department

Serves four to six. Roland says this is another of his father's great recipes.

2 pounds broccoli, stemmed and cut into bite-size pieces

6 tablespoons olive oil

6 tablespoons lemon juice

2 medium garlic cloves, crushed

salt to taste

pepper to taste

Cook the broccoli in salted water just until tender.

Drain and chill thoroughly.

Combine olive oil, lemon juice, and garlic. Drizzle dressing over broccoli right before eating.

Salt and pepper to taste. Enjoy!

colorado corn packets

Mick Rosacci, Tony's Meats & Specialty Foods

Serves four to six. This is a great way to grill those vegetables.

1-2 mild green chilies

4 large ears of corn

4 slices bacon, diced

1/4 sweet red pepper, minced

salt

pepper

butter

1 green onion, thinly sliced

If using fresh green chili, roast over a hot grill. Place in a paper bag until cool enough to handle. Then scrape off the skin, remove the seeds and mince.

Cut the kernels from the ears of corn and place in a bowl with bacon, bell pepper and green chili.

Mound the mixture on half of a two-foot sheet of foil, leaving a one-inch border on the sides; sprinkle with salt and pepper and dot with butter.

Fold the other half of the foil over the corn and seal the edges well by repeated crimping.

Grill over low-to-medium coals, turning regularly, for six-to-ten minutes or until packet is puffed. Open the packet at the table and sprinkle with green onion just before serving.

ÿ Bill Decker ÿ

Bill Decker, International Entrepreneur

Partners International, Inc.

When it comes to comments about food, Bill Decker doesn't mince words. Here is his tip for impressing a special lady, "There is nothing a woman likes more then a nice meal, low candlelight, and good atmosphere, with wine." Add a stand-up comedy act to that recipe and you are describing Bill Decker himself.

Bill is a business traveler with an interesting hobby— learning how to cook the cuisine of the country he is visiting. So far he has mastered dishes from seventy countries. He says, "India is one place I just could not get into the kitchen. Due to the class system, women do not invite men into their kitchens to cook. The culture just does not allow for this to happen."

He recalls how, at the age of twenty-three, hearing that you could live in Taiwan on $200 a month, he grabbed his suitcase, his mandolin, a one-way ticket and headed out. He says: "I learned things there I never would have encountered if I had stayed in the United States. I later applied them to business."

Bill, his wife, stepson, and new daughter now live in Lakewood, Colorado. He is still a traveler but also devotes time and talent to family. Besides running a consulting practice, he teaches international business and entrepreneurship at MBA programs in Denver.

incredibly healthy hummus with fatoush

Bill Decker, Partners International, Inc.

Eat hummus with your hands by tearing warm pita into bite-size pieces. Use it to scoop beans off the plate. As with Eastern cultures, Bill says, the meal is a great way to connect and is a very social way of doing business. Add some wine and the evening is set for that special date. Better get the breath mints ready though....

"In many countries a meal is often eaten before any kind of business transaction takes place. Many important decisions are made over a plate of cuisine. As a matter of fact 'Hello' in Chinese is, 'Have you eaten yet?'"

—Bill Decker

1/2 pound lean chopped steak, optional

1/2 cup parsley, chopped, divided

6 cloves garlic, divided

12 cardamom pods, cracked

2 cans garbanzo beans (chick peas)

1 cucumber diced

4 romano tomatoes

2 lemons, divided

zatar

2 tablespoons cumin

1 lime, divided

mediterranean-style olives

extra virgin olive oil

paprika

to taste salt and pepper

1/3 cup pine nuts

pita pocket bread, cut in half

tahini, optional

Brown the beef; Add two tablespoons of the parsley, one garlic clove and cracked cardamom pods. Meanwhile, drain the garbanzo beans and rinse very well. Cover the beans with water and cook for about twenty-five minutes, until the skins separate from the beans.

For the Fatoush: Dice the unpeeled cucumber, and mix with the remaining parsley, juice from half a lemon and olive oil. Add Zatar and cumin. Mix and refrigerate until hummus and meat are done.

Drain the garbanzo beans, reserving the liquid from the cooking process. Blend two-thirds of the garbanzo beans with remainder of garlic cloves and juice from the remainder one and a half lemons, a pinch of Zatar, one-third of the lime juice, two tablespoons sea salt or to taste and cumin to taste. Blend to the consistency of spackle. Add some of the remaining beans and blend slightly to add texture. Use the liquid from cooking the beans to thin during blending process if needed.

Take the cardamom and garlic out of the meat. Spread hummus and beans on a plate and decorate with parsley. Sprinkle olive oil, paprika, Zatar, and olives on top of the beans. Top with pine nuts. Add remaining cooked beans and sprinkle with cumin and lace the beef across the top. Add a few scoops of tahini if desired. (Make tahini paste with tahini, lemon and olive oil.) This dish is hearty—and salty. Time to ignore the doctor!

ÿ Michael Comstedt ÿ

pommes berny

Michael Comstedt, Executive Chef, Cook Street School of Fine Cooking

Yields eight servings. This is one of the many recipes used to teach culinary students at Cook Street School of Fine Cooking. Quenelles are a kind of delicate forcemeat, commonly poached and used as a dish by itself or for garnishing.

6 medium - large potatoes in the skins

2 teaspoons butter

1 cup half and half, heated

sea salt

fresh ground pepper

nutmeg

1-2 beaten eggs

peanut oil

for coating

1/2 cup almonds, ground,

1 cup bread crumbs

1/2 cup chopped parsley

4 eggs, beaten

flour

Put whole potatoes in their skins, in a pot of cold water. Cook them until they are knife tender, about forty-five minutes. Remove from the water, peel and rice them. Mix in the butter and hot half and half to make a smooth puree; season with salt, pepper and nutmeg.

Incorporate a beaten egg into the potatoes to bind the mixture. If the potatoes seem very stiff, add a second beaten egg. Form the potatoes into large quenelles with two large spoons. Combine the almonds, bread crumbs and parsley in a medium bowl. Dust the quenelles in flour; dip into the beaten eggs and coat with the almond mixture. Set on a buttered baking sheet.

Heat a large pot of peanut oil to about 375 degrees. Preheat oven to 350 degrees.

Fry the quenelles in the hot peanut oil until golden brown. Remove from the oil and return to the baking sheet. Heat in the oven to warm before serving, if necessary.

Michael Comstedt on the left with Phillip Waters on the right, a student of Cook Street School of Fine Cooking

Michael Comstedt C.E.C., C.C.E., Executive Chef and School Director

Cook Street School of Fine Cooking

Walking into Cook Street School of Fine Cooking, you get the feeling that this is where it all starts. The atmosphere is all about professional pursuits and the smells are exquisite. The students are attentive as they listen to their certified culinary educator, Michael Comstedt, and get hands-on training. More than likely, with Michael as their instructor, they are learning about Italian and French cuisine and good wines.

Michael inherited his culinary inclinations from his grandfather. He's worked at the Westin Hotel chain and then Green Briar Inn for fifteen years where, under his leadership, the inn received the Wine Spectator Award of Excellence and the Mobil Travel Guide's Four Star rating.

Michael is a Certified Executive Chef and a trained sommelier, He also was instrumental in developing the Professional Culinary Arts Program at the Cooking School of the Rockies in Boulder. This chef is smitten with passion for his work and it shows.

Peter Ryan & Chris Caldes cooking up some head cheese at the Cook Street School of Fine Cooking.

samfaina

Michael Comstedt, Cook Street School of Fine Cooking

Yields six-to-eight servings. Samfaina can also be used as a sauce. Cook longer, adding water if necessary, until the mixture has attained a marmalade-like consistency and the vegetables have lost their shape.

4 one-and-a-half pound japanese eggplants

1/2 pound red peppers

8 medium tomatoes

1/2 pounds onions

2/3 cup extra virgin olive oil

4 cloves garlic, minced

1 tablespoon honey

4 tablespoons vinegar

salt and pepper

Cut the eggplant into one-inch cubes, leaving the skins on. Roast the red peppers: peel, seed and cut into one-inch cubes. Peel, seed and chop the tomatoes. Halve the onion and cut into one-inch cubes.

Over medium-high, heat enough oil to cover the bottom of the pan. Add the eggplant and caramelize one side before stirring. Once the eggplant is nice and caramelized on all sides, add the garlic and sauté quickly until fragrant. Remove the eggplant and garlic to a bowl and reserve.

Add a little more oil to the sauté pan and, when hot, add the onions. Sauté onions until soft, then add the reserved eggplant, tomatoes and peppers. Reduce the heat and simmer uncovered until liquid has evaporated and vegetables are soft. Mix the honey and vinegar together and add to the vegetables. Season with salt and pepper.

butter mushrooms with port

Christopher S. Grosz, Littleton Police Department

Serves four. The port wine makes this a unique and delightful side dish.

2 shallots

4 cloves garlic

1 stick butter

1 cup port

2 twenty-four ounce containers of mushrooms

1 bunch italian parsley

salt to taste

pepper to taste

Mince the garlic and shallots. Melt the butter in a large skillet and add the garlic and shallots. Cook over medium heat until almost transparent.

Add the port wine; mix well. Clean the mushrooms and add them whole. Cook over medium-high heat while stirring frequently.

Dice the parsley, leaves only. Add just before the mushrooms are done. Salt and pepper to taste.

Brian E.P.B. O'Connell, N.M.D., Medical Director

Mountain Area Naturopathic Associates (MANA Clinic)

Brian O'Connell is a second generation Irishman from Limerick, Ireland, who loves to cook and has thirteen years in herbs and nutrition. Interestingly, Brian attributes his skill in the kitchen as a foundation for his interest in chemistry and forensics. "Coming from a family of cooks," Brian adds, "I learned how to cook from scratch using good, nutritious ingredients to create my meals."

Through his background in pharmaceutics and toxicology, he witnessed first-hand the deleterious effects of some medications. In his clinic, he does not prescribe man-made drugs, but rather makes his own treatments. As a doctor of naturopathic medicine, Brian says he has a passion for sharing knowledge and assisting people in being healthy.

When not at the clinic or with family, he sings for others with his smooth second tenor voice. He is also learning the bagpipes.

ℨ *Brian E.P.B. O'Connell* ℨ

artichokes al canzano

Brian O'Connell, NMD, Mountain Area Naturopathic Associates

Serves six to eight. Brian says, "Use a dark enamel lobster pot to cook the artichokes as the dark colors heat faster than the white." Yes, he uses three heads of garlic in this recipe.

4 large fresh lemons, juiced

2-3 cups extra virgin olive oil

coarse sea salt to taste

coarse pepper to taste

3 heads of garlic

8 large artichokes with as little purple color as possible

3 bunches of italian parsley, chopped, stems and all

In a large bowl combine the juice of the lemons, olive oil, salt and pepper. Mix well.

Clean garlic and break them into cloves. Remove stems from artichokes so the body of the artichoke rests flat on the cutting board. Trim stems of all dried areas and pickers and soak the artichokes in the oil/lemon for a few minutes.

Cut a quarter inch across the top of each artichoke to remove thorns off the crown of the 'choke. With kitchen shears or a paring knife. Remove all other exterior from the body of the 'choke. Open the top of the 'choke with both thumbs. Be careful as the interior is loaded with thorns. Once open, stuff the 'chokes with the parsley and four-to-five cloves of garlic per 'choke. There is no such thing as too much garlic! Place the stuffed chokes in the lobster pot and cover with enough water so that nine-tenths of the 'chokes are submerged. Drizzle oil/lemon mixture over all 'chokes, being sure to get the insides of all. Put stems in the pot as well—they are also edible. Add more salt and pepper at this stage.

Cover, turn on the heat and let steam/boil for five-to-six hours, checking every hour. Be sure to keep the water level up, as the 'chokes will cook dry otherwise.

Remove each with a large spoon and serve.

energy bars

Donald J. Tallman, Augustana Arts

The "add-ins" listed in the ingredients can be any combination of coconut, unsalted nuts, raisins, chocolate or carob chips, and chopped dried fruit that adds up to one or two cups. Donald uses this recipe as a quick pick-me-up after working out. He says it tastes better than store-bought and is not filled with all those preservatives.

1 cup honey

3/4 cup smooth peanut butter

1 cup orange juice

2 -1/2 cups rolled oats

1/2 cup wheat germ

3/4 cup vanilla soy powder, approximately 60 mg. protein

1 cup whole wheat flour

1 teaspoon baking soda

1 tablespoon cinnamon

1 teaspoon cloves

1 teaspoon nutmeg

1-2 cups add-ins

Preheat oven to 350 degrees. Mix honey and peanut butter in a bowl until well blended. Add orange juice and mix.

Stir in oats, wheat germ, soy powder, flour, baking soda, spices and dried fruit or other add-ins. If too dry, add more orange juice, a splash at a time. If it is too sticky, add oats one tablespoon at a time. The mixture should be a bit sticky.

Spoon the mixture into a 9" x 13" lightly greased pan and bake for fifteen-to-twenty minutes. When done, it will still be soft but slightly browned.

Cut into twelve segments and let cool. Once cool, place each bar in an individual plastic bag for storage. These can also be frozen.

Donald Tallman, Executive Director

Augustana Arts

From cooking to community involvement, Donald Tallman is genuinely interested in people and his life centers on them. As the executive director of Augustana Arts, Donald creates cultural experiences, producing and presenting regional and international groups such as the Moscow Chamber Orchestra, Indian sitarist Kartik Seshadri, and the I Musici de Montreal Chamber Orchestra. "I touch a lot of people and get paid for it," is how he succinctly characterizes his work.

Donald began cooking when he was a graduate student. Tired of eating out, he discovered cooking was enjoyable. He could not afford taking dates to a restaurant at the time, so he cooked for them.

Today, Donald not only does all the cooking at home, but he does the grocery shopping as well. Who wouldn't want this man around their house? He says, "Cooking for a family is about connecting." His wonderful recipes are his own creations.

Donald adds that the creative expression you make with your voice is also a wonderful thing. Just like cooking, singing is a creative process in which you have an emotional impact. Donald performs solo as a professional tenor—he's sung at Temple Emanuel on high holy days and also at Rockies home games belting out the National Anthem.

ÿ *Donald Tallman* ÿ

portabello, smoked gouda and red pepper panini

Donald J. Tallman, Augustana Arts

Serves four. Three tablespoons fresh, chopped basil can be substituted for the dried. Fresh is always better, says Donald, and gives that homey touch.

2 eight-ounce packages sliced portabello mushroom caps

1 sliced red onion

olive oil

1/2 cup mayonnaise

1 teaspoon dried basil

1 loaf – focaccia bread

2 cups roasted red peppers

4 slices smoked gouda cheese

In large covered skillet, sauté onion and mushrooms until onions are soft; remove to a bowl. In a separate bowl, combine mayonnaise and basil.

Split the focaccia loaf in half horizontally and cut vertically into four large sandwiches.

On each sandwich, spread mayonnaise/basil mixture. Add slice of gouda, one-half cup peppers, one-half cup mushroom/onion mixture. Replace the top of the bread on each.

Drizzle olive oil on both sides of bread. Reheat the skillet. Place sandwiches in hot skillet and heat on both sides until golden brown.

goat cheese & potato custard

Mark D. Black, Executive Chef, Brown Palace Hotel

Serves eight. This recipe has a unique flavor that will delight guests. It can be prepared ahead and baked right before serving.

1 ounce butter, melted

3 russet potatoes, peeled and medium diced

salt and pepper to taste

6 large eggs

4 ounces milk

ground nutmeg to taste

8 ounces goat cheese

2 tablespoons fresh chives, sliced

Toss the potatoes in the butter. Spread the potatoes on a sheet pan, season with salt and pepper. Roast at 350 degrees until tender, approximately twenty-five minutes.

Whisk together the eggs and milk. Season the mixture with salt and pepper and a dash of nutmeg.

Crumble the goat cheese over the potatoes and sprinkle with the chives. Divide the potato mixture among eight buttered, four-fluid-ounce soufflé dishes. Divide the custard among the dishes. Bake at 300 degrees until set, approximately forty minutes. Remove from the oven and serve immediately.

David Veal, Veal Creative

David Veal, a native of Golden, Colorado, like any good cook, he exercised his creative juices early in life. While other boys were out playing sports he was drawing spacecrafts, writing songs and short stories, and dreaming of possibilities. His need to create merged with his love of discovery. This is reflected in his work as a graphic artist, and in the unusual, sometimes hazardous, dishes he prepares for his family at home. His believes in having fun while seeking out alternative approaches to everything life has to offer. "Life offers a series of mistakes and innovations. Without allowing yourself to make mistakes you lose the opportunity to discover great things."

David began to take his home cooking seriously in college when he read *Eat to Win*, a well-publicized 'ultimate health' cookbook that was endorsed by Martina Navratilova in the early 1980's. "That idea of eating the right food and running my five miles a day gave me focus during those years; it was almost like a spiritual thing at the time."

David creates his possibilities in the Highlands Ranch area with wife Patti, his son Jeremy, and his father-in-law Gene Howard.

ÿ *David Veal* ÿ

linguini and artichoke

David Veal, Veal Creative

Four servings. David says: "Cooking is an extension of my creativity. But, like illustrations, sometimes you get a long time to do your work and sometimes it has to be done fast. Whatever, it still needs to be good."

2 tablespoons olive oil

2 cloves garlic, chopped

1 medium tomato, diced

2 cups chopped carrots

1/2 yellow bell pepper, diced

1 cup green beans, chopped

8 ounces linguini

1 eight-ounce can artichoke hearts

1 cup cooking wine

butter

4 slices fresh sourdough bread

1/4 cup grated sharp cheddar

to taste garlic salt

1/2 cup sliced almonds

1/2 cup sliced olives

1/3 cup feta cheese

to taste basil, optional

Heat olive oil in a skillet on medium heat. Add garlic and simmer for a few minutes. Add chopped vegetables. Prepare the linguini.

Add the artichoke hearts and the wine to the vegetables. Let this simmer on medium heat for approximately fifteen minutes, stirring occasionally. The idea is to let the tomato and artichokes soften, blending their tastes into the wine and oil, yet leaving some body to the carrots, pepper and green beans.

Butter both sides of the sourdough bread and place on a cookie sheet. Sprinkle with the cheddar cheese and garlic salt. Place under the broiler for two minutes or less, depending on how well the cheese melts. Take out the toast and sprinkle on the almonds. Lightly press the almonds into the cheese. Optional: add a sprinkle of basil.

The linguini can be positioned to the side of the plate or used as a bed for the vegetables.

To the vegetables add additional garlic salt to taste, the olives and the feta cheese. Turn the heat off and give the feta a moment to settle in. Add the vegetables and a good slice of garlic bread to the plate and serve.

Jon R. Tandler, Attorney at Law

Isaacson, Rosenbaum, Woods & Levy

Here is another romantic gentleman—on the first date he had with the woman who would become his wife, he cooked for her. He and his two brothers learned to cook from family and Scouts—"simply because we wanted to, had to, liked to cook," he says.

Jon specializes in proprietary rights, authors, publishing and software companies, anyone dealing with copyrights, trademarks and registration issues. His sound guidance protects those who seek his counsel. Jon is a shareholder of Isaacson, Rosenbaum, Woods & Levy.

Jon enjoys working and puts in long hours, but "my free time I spend with my family, exercise and read." Walking with a friend, hiking with family and friends and snowshoeing in the winter help to balance out a work schedule that can sometimes get pretty stressful.

After studying for an entire year, in 2003 at the age of forty-six, Jon became a Bar Mitzvah. Jon completed his studies and fulfilled a desire from his youth. It is never too late to fulfill dreams.

papa chinese

Jon R. Tandler, Isaacson, Attorney at Law, Rosenbaum, Woods & Levy

Serves four. Jon says, "This is the one my children always ask me to make."

2 large broccoli bunches

1 large bok choy

12-15 scallions

2 twelve-ounce packages firm tofu

2 five-ounce packages fresh spinach

vegetable oil

2 eight-ounce packages fresh bean sprouts

1 eight-ounce cans water chestnuts

brown or white rice

garlic powder

low-salt soy sauce or organic whole soybean wheat-free soy sauce

Wash all of the vegetables. Cut broccoli in long-stemmed florets. Cut bok choy in three inch long pieces using the leaf also. Cut the scallions lengthwise into thin strands, and then cut the strands into approximately three-inch pieces

Steam broccoli and bok choy in sauce pan or steamer until firm but not mushy.

Cut tofu in quarter-inch thick squares. Braise tofu with vegetable oil, garlic powder and soy sauce in wok or large sauté pan. Make sure you use a large wok or pan so that you have ample room for the above ingredients.

Add broccoli, bok choy, bean sprouts, scallions, water chestnuts and spinach so that the spinach is on top. Stir-fry until spinach is steamed/cooked down and everything is cooked in; season with garlic powder and soy sauce. Should be about fifteen minutes of stir-frying.

Cook rice according to directions on package.

Optional: You also could use snow peas, string beans, mushrooms, cauliflower, and cabbage; sesame oil on the side, not cooked in; rice noodles instead of rice.

Ÿ *Jon Tandler* Ÿ

spicy grilled corn on the cob

Eric Chester, Generation Why

Eric's recipes are as creative his work.

8 ears corn

1/2 cup grated cotija cheese

4 fresh limes, quartered

2 tablespoons chives, chopped for garnish

for garlic butter:

2 sticks unsalted butter, slightly softened

8 cloves of garlic, peeled and coarsely chopped

1/4 habanero pepper, seeded

1/4 bunch chives

salt and freshly ground pepper

Peel back the husks of the corn without removing them. Remove the silk and re-cover the corn with the husk. Soak in a large bowl of cold water for thirty minutes.

For the garlic butter: Combine the butter, garlic, habanero pepper and chives in a food processor and process until smooth. Season with salt and pepper and set aside until ready to use.

Preheat grill to medium. Remove the corn from the water and shake off excess water. Place the corn on the grill, close the cover and grill for fifteen-to-twenty minutes. Unwrap the corn and brush with the garlic butter; sprinkle with the Cotija cheese and a squeeze of lime juice. Sprinkle with chives. Serve and enjoy!

spinach-cheese quiche

Donald J. Tallman, Augustana Arts

Serves four to six. For that quiche lover, this is a tasty meal.

1 ten-ounce package chopped frozen spinach

1 onion chopped

1 teaspoon olive oil

3/4 cup cottage cheese

1/3 cup shredded parmesan cheese

1/3 cup shredded monterey jack cheese

1/3 cup crumbled feta cheese

4 eggs

1/2 teaspoon nutmeg

1/2 teaspoon dill weed

1 deep-dish frozen pie crust

Preheat oven to 350 degrees.

In the microwave, cook the spinach in the package for four minutes to thaw. Remove the spinach from the package and squeeze out in a colander until dry.

Heat oil in a large skillet and sauté onions two or three minutes over medium heat.

Add spinach and cook for four minutes.

Meanwhile, in a food processor or mixer, combine cottage cheese, eggs and spices until well blended while spinach and onions are cooking. Pour the cottage cheese and egg mixture in a large bowl.

Add rest of cheeses, spinach and onions and stir until blended.

Pour mixture into frozen pie crust and bake for one hour or until top is golden brown.

Nick Moschetti, Chef and Manager

Bisetti's Ristorante

Nick Moschetti's love for the culinary arts makes him a true catch for any eligible bachelorette. We'd say a woman would love to have this chef around the house. You can thank his mother. Nick got his first lessons and passion for fine food from her.

Nick decided to make culinary arts a career while working as a line cook at Bisetti's Ristorante in Fort Collins, Colorado. He rounded out his education with a degree from the Art Institute of Colorado and now works as head chef and co-manages Bisetti's in Highlands Ranch with owner Michael Sagrillo.

Passion is the one ingredient that drives all good chefs. Nick says, "Food is more then eating, it is an experience; only a true chef would agree." He has been known to cook a good meal or two for a date, although he says he chooses carefully who shall taste his delicacies.

spinach, artichoke and asparagus salad

Nicholas Moschetti, Chef and Manager, Bisetti's Ristorante

Serves four to eight. This professional chef likes to create culinary delights for family and friends. He says: "This is a great cold summer salad that doubles as a veggie dish. I served it at a family barbecue and everyone loved it!" Oh yes, he always prefers fresh herbs to dry.

1 can artichoke hearts

1 pound fresh asparagus

1 clove garlic, minced

1 small shallot, minced

3 ounces balsamic vinegar

1 teaspoon dijon mustard

1 teaspoon honey

9 ounces extra virgin olive oil

1 pinch basil, fresh or dry

1 pinch thyme, fresh or dry

1 pinch rosemary, fresh or dry

1 pinch parsley, fresh or dry

salt and black pepper to taste

3 ounces fresh baby spinach

1/4 cup fresh grated parmesan or romano cheese

Prepare the asparagus by cutting off the lower third or where it naturally breaks off each spear. Bring a large pot of heavily salted water to a boil to blanch the asparagus. Fill a separate bowl with ice water. Quarter and drain the artichoke hearts.

While your water is coming to a boil, prepare the vinaigrette: In a medium stainless steel bowl whisk together garlic, shallot, vinegar, mustard, and honey. Slowly drizzle in the olive oil in a narrow stream while at the same time whisking. It helps to place a damp towel under the bowl so it doesn't spin while you're pouring and whisking. The vinaigrette should thicken and lighten in color when the oil is added. Then add herbs and salt and pepper to taste.

Once the water has reached a full rolling boil, add asparagus. Blanch the asparagus for about three-to-five minutes, or until slightly tender, but still crisp.

Remove asparagus from the water and place immediately into the ice water to stop the cooking. Add the asparagus and artichoke hearts to the vinaigrette and allow to marinate in the fridge for an hour or two for the best flavor.

Before serving, toss the spinach with the asparagus, artichoke hearts, dressing and parmesan cheese.

ÿ **Nick Moschetti** ÿ

jicama citrus salad

Christopher S. Grosz, Littleton Police Department

Serves four. Chris says he likes Auslese white wine for this recipe.

4 pounds jicama, unpeeled

1 bunch cilantro

1 small red onion

10 ounces grape tomatoes

12 ounces honey

1 cup sweet white wine

1 cup orange juice

1 tablespoon red pepper flakes

1/2 tablespoon kosher salt

Peel the jicama and cut it into french fry-sized pieces. Place it in a large mixing bowl.

Clean and roughly dice the cilantro and add to the jicama.

Slice the onion into thin slices and add.

Clean the tomatoes, cut in halves and add.

In a separate, smaller bowl, mix the honey, wine, orange juice, red pepper flakes and kosher salt. Mix well.

Pour the liquid over the jicama mixture and mix well.

stir-fried zucchini & yellow squash

Candis Kloverstrom, Illustrator & Author

The author says, "Ok, I couldn't resist putting in one of my own recipes. I love clam juice, rosemary and feta cheese. So, I combined them into this stir-fry vegetable dish. Be careful how much rosemary you use. A little goes a long way. I personally like its flavor."

2 shallots

4 small yellow squash

4 small zucchini

1/3 cup clam juice

1 tablespoon fresh rosemary or to taste

1/3 cup crumbled feta cheese

kosher salt to taste

coarse ground black pepper to taste

Cut the shallots julienne style. Clean and cut the unpeeled squash and zucchini into three-inch julienne strips. The end result depends upon the peeling being left on. (It is better for you anyway.)

Using a wok, sauté the shallots in the clam juice until almost transparent.

Add the yellow squash first; then on top of that place the zucchini. Sprinkle the feta cheese and rosemary over the top. Cover for about five minutes until the vegetables are just done, yet firm. Too much time will make the vegetables limp and ruin the dish.

Mix just long enough to blend in the cheese, about thirty seconds or so. This dish is best if the cheese is still a little chunky. In fact, you can add a little extra at the end to give it that cheesy texture. Salt and pepper to taste.

Randy James, DC

Twin Peaks Chiropractic, P.C.

Dr. Randy James developed his culinary interests watching his grandmother make Potica (pronounced poteetza). He recalls how she kneaded the dough, rolling it extra thin, shaping it into this delicious dessert. Many of Randy's dishes are from traditional family recipes. Today, preparing these dishes brings back fond memories of the care and attention that his grandmother put into each meal.

Randy is innovative in his cooking and in his chiropractic practice. Both he and his wife are chiropractors and know good nutrition is the secret to good health. Not surprisingly, some of his best dishes are organic delights.

"Grandmothers are special people; learning at their knees, listening to stories from days gone by, passing those tidbits on to future generations are values that shape our lives."

—*Dr. Randy James*

ÿ *Randy James* ÿ

fried spaghetti

Dr. Randy James

This recipe is great for those spaghetti and veggie fans.

1 stick butter or 1/2 cup olive oil

2-3 stalks celery

10-12 medium fresh mushrooms

1 small zucchini

1 medium bell pepper, green or red

1 small onion

1 small tomato, cut into small chunks

few pitted black olives

seasoning salt to taste

1 pound thin spaghetti, cooked and drained

salt & garlic pepper to taste

parmesan cheese

Slice all vegetables into one-quarter or one-half inch pieces.

Using a large, non-stick skillet, sauté vegetables starting with celery. Then add mushrooms, zucchini, peppers and onion until all are barely soft, about two-to-three minutes total.

Add the tomato and black olives. Sauté an additional minute. Add the seasoning salt (Randy suggests Morton's Nature seasoning salt) and garlic pepper to taste as you sauté.

Add hot cooked spaghetti and sauté another minute. Toss with Parmesan cheese and serve.

delicious hors d'oeuvres & sinful desserts

aji colombian empanadas • empanada dough • easy apple cobbler • meat empanadas • pepper poppers • chocolate terrine with espresso & berries • chambord berry dessert sauce • baked pears • tasty cheesecake • lobster wontons • simple chili relleños • lebanese baklava • chinese chicken wings • vanilla or chocolate custard ice cream • hard sauce • cinnamon cranberry bread pudding • blueberry fried cheesecake • brad's killer buffalo wings • white chocolate mousse • walnut potica • lefsa • steve kelley's favorite palacsinta

ÿ **David Aylmer** ÿ

aji colombian empanadas

David Aylmer, Chef

Chartwell's at Johnson & Wales University

David Aylmer, Chartwell's at Johnson & Wales University

This is a delightful Colombian version empanada dish that is great as an appetizer or while you are watching your favorite sport.

1-1/2 pounds plum tomatoes

3/4 cup finely chopped white onion

1/2 cup chopped fresh cilantro leaves

1 tablespoon fresh lime juice

2 tablespoons minced, seeded jalapeño or serrano chilies

1 teaspoon minced garlic clove

1/2 teaspoon salt

pinch cayenne

empanada dough, page 152

Dice, seed and core the tomatoes. Combine all of the ingredients in a bowl and stir well. Cover and allow to rest at room temperature for one hour for the flavors to blend.

Place a spoonful of filling in the center of each circle of pastry. Fold over the pastry and seal the edges with water. Let the empanadas rest in the refrigerator for a half hour or freeze immediately. Bake the frozen empanadas without defrosting.

Empanadas may be glazed with one egg and two tablespoons milk. Combine the milk and egg, beat well and glaze the empanadas. Bake until golden in a 400-degree oven for about fifteen minutes. Or they may be deep fried in oil at 375 degrees until golden brown, one-to-two minutes per side. If you deep-fry them, make sure the edges are well sealed so the filling won't leak.

Life does not simply unfold, we know. More often than not, life happenings dictate our career paths. This was certainly true for Dave Aylmer. His initial inclination had been criminal law enforcement. As an intern for the California Department of Justice Bureau of Narcotics he enjoyed stakeouts and researching cases. Then, during one stakeout, someone was killed. This unfortunate event became one of the deciding factors in David's decision to follow his true passion: a career in the culinary arts.

As the executive chef of Johnson & Wales University's Chartwell's Catering, David spends most days managing his kitchen and staff. Asked about the success of his students, he says, "It is my goal to help my staff be everything they can be. I first seek out those who want to move up and show interest and reliability in their work. I will do everything I can to empower them to advance." David's other goal is making the Johnson & Wales cafeteria a working kitchen where the culinary students receive first-hand training, creating a culinary experience for all.

empanada dough

David Aylmer, Chartwell's at Johnson & Wales University

There are those who have their secret formula for making this dough. Try your hand at David Aylmer's.

2 cups flour

1/2 cup lard

2 -1/2 tablespoons unsalted butter

1/2 cup iced water, approximately

In a large bowl, combine the flour with the lard, butter and salt. Mix lightly with your fingertips until the dough forms grape-sized pieces. You should still be able to see streaks of fat.

Stir in the water. Lightly knead, handling the dough as little as possible, until the dough forms a ball. Add a little more water if needed.

Refrigerate for at least one hour, then remove and let it return to room temperature for about one hour before rolling. The dough can be frozen for up to a week.

Pinch off about half the dough. Roll it out on a floured surface to a thickness of one-eighth inch. Cut out three circles. about six inches in diameter. Then, gather the scraps, add to the rest of the dough, and roll out another batch of circles. Repeat with the rest of the scraps. This should be enough dough for about twenty-four empanadas.

easy apple cobbler

Richard Kemerling, Prime-Sight Associates, dba Pearle Vision

Serves four to six. This is a great last-minute dessert item.

4 cups sliced apples, with or without skins

1-2 tablespoons lemon juice

1 box of your favorite white cake mix

1 cup brown sugar

1/4 cup raisins, optional

1/2 teaspoon ground cinnamon

1 stick butter or margarine, melted

vanilla ice cream

Preheat oven to 350 degrees. Wash the fruit well and slice. As you are coring the fruit, place slices in a large bowl half full of water with the lemon juice. This will keep your apple slices from turning brown until you are finished slicing.

Spread half the drained sliced fruit in the bottom of a 9" x 12" non-stick baking pan or a well-oiled baking dish. Sprinkle half of the dry cake mix over the fruit. Sprinkle the raisins over the top of the mixture.

Spread the remaining fruit slices evenly on top of this. Sprinkle the rest of the dry cake mix on top of this. Sprinkle on cinnamon to taste. Crumble the brown sugar evenly over the top of the mixture. Dribble the melted butter or margarine evenly over that.

Bake the cobbler at 350 degrees for approximately fifty-to-sixty minutes or until top is golden brown. Serve hot with vanilla ice cream.

Alternative: Mix half the brown sugar with the apples, lemon juice and raisins. Combine softened butter, cake mix and cinnamon to form a crumbly mixture. Then sprinkle over the top of the apples for a nice topping.

**Marcelo Balboa,
Soccer Professional**

Marcelo Balboa is a soccer analyst for HD Net TV, a club coach for the Broomfield Blast, and the second assistant coach for the Colorado School of Mines, but he's making time for his two sons these days. "When I was on the road with soccer," Marcelo says, "my oldest hardly knew me. Today that is different. I enjoy doing what I never had a chance to do then—be with my kids."

Previously Marcelo played for the US National Team and the Colorado Rapids, and was dubbed the five-time all-star team member in four consecutive years. He also was athlete of the year twice and named "Iron Man" by the American press.

So, how did this world-famous athlete start his culinary pursuits? Like a lot of the gentlemen in this book, it was college that got him cooking. Just to have something to eat, it was a case of learning how to cook, eating poorly or starve. Today Marcelo brings an exotic flavor to some of his dishes, using recipes from Argentina, his homeland.

meat empanadas

Marcelo L. Balboa, soccer professional

Marcelo watched his mother prepare this recipe. Today, he fixes this for his own family and friends. Tapas are the size of corn tostadas only they are made with a flour mixture. As an Argentinian recipe, they can be purchased at the El Azteca, 303-893-3642 or try the dough recipe on page 152.

1 1/2 pounds ground beef

2 hard-boiled eggs

7 - 8 green olives

1 small onion

salt and pepper to taste

2 dozen empanada tapas

vegetable oil

Brown the ground beef in a frying pan; drain all excess fat. Peel and dice the eggs. Chop the onion and green olives into small pieces.

Add the eggs, olives and onions to the meat; salt and pepper to taste. Heat the entire mixture on medium to high.

Wet the edges of the tapa dough with a little water. Add about three tablespoons of the meat mixture. Fold in half. Using a fork, seal the edges of the empanada by pressing down on the dough leaving a fork-mark all around the outside.

Deep-fat fry each empanada at 450 degrees until both sides are lightly browned, not burnt. Let cool on a paper towel to drain any excess oil.

As a variation of the meat mixture: Substitute shredded mozzarella cheese with strips of lean ham for the ground hamburger. Chicken can also be used rather than the ground hamburger.

ÿ *Marcelo Balboa* ÿ

Mark Gagnon,
Director of Operations

Cognitive Solutions

Like other men who like to cook, Mark Gagnon uses cooking as his stress reliever. Originally, he began concocting meals in the Boy Scouts; today he uses cooking to bless his wife and friends. Sharing the meal preparation duties with his wife, Michelle, Mark relies on the recipes handed down from past generations.

The Gagnon's, originally from New Hampshire, may host a New England style in their home, but the atmosphere sizzles with classic rock salting the air. During the day Mark is the Director of Operations for Cognitive Solutions, a world-wide manufacturer of thermal label printing solutions and supplies headquartered in Golden, Colorado.

ÿ *Mark Gagnon* ÿ

pepper poppers

Mark A. Gagnon, Cognitive Solutions

Serves at least four-to-six people, depending on appetites and the number of other hors d'oeuvres you are serving. This can be as hot or mild as desired.

1 pound fresh jalapeños

1 eight-ounce package cream cheese, softened

1 cup shredded sharp cheddar cheese

1 cup shredded monterey jack cheese

6 bacon strips, cooked, crumbled

1/4 teaspoon salt

1/4 teaspoon chili powder

1/4 teaspoon garlic powder

1/2 cup dry bread crumbs

Cut the jalapeños in half and seed. Wear gloves while handling them.

In mixing bowl, combine the cheeses, bacon and seasonings; mix well.

Spoon filling into each pepper half.

Roll in breadcrumbs. Place on a greased 15" x 10" cookie sheet.

Bake, uncovered, at 325 degrees. The longer the baking time, the milder the bite. Bake thirty minutes for spicy, forty minutes for medium and fifty minutes for mild.

chocolate terrine with espresso and berries

Stephen Kleinman, Executive Chef, Colorado Convention Center

Here's another good one.

16 ounces semisweet chocolate

1 cup heavy whipping cream

1/2 cup filbert nuts (hazelnuts)

4 ounces unsalted butter

3 cups espresso coffee

1 cup water

16 egg yolks

1 pound sugar

1 pint raspberries

Melt chocolate in a double boiler. Roast the filberts in a 350-degree oven for twenty minutes and peel off the skins. Coarsely chop the nuts.

When the chocolate is melted, about 185 degrees on a candy thermometer, whisk in the butter. Then the cream. Note, the chocolate will goop up a bit, but it will smooth out as you add more liquid. Add the chopped nuts. Then turn this out into an eight-inch loaf pan that is lined with wax paper or parchment paper. Let it cool in the refrigerator until the chocolate is solid.

For the sauce: Bring the espresso and water to a boil. In a seperate bowl, whisk the eggs and sugar until the eggs have absorbed all of the sugar.

Pour a small amount of the hot espresso at a time into the egg mixture to temper the eggs; then add all of the egg mixture to the rest of the espresso and bring it to a boil. Strain immediately and cool, placing parchment paper on top of the mix so it does not form a skin.

To serve: Run knife under hot water and wipe off. Then cut chocolate terrine into one-quarter inch slices. Pour sauce on a plate; lay the sliced terrine on top and sprinkle with the berries. Enjoy!

chambord berry dessert sauce

Christopher S. Grosz, Littleton Police Department

This is a great item to keep in your refrigerator if you are an ice-cream-with-topping fan.

1/2 cup chambord liqueur

1 twelve-ounce jar red currant jelly

**1 eighteen-ounce jar
red raspberry preserves**

1/4 tablespoon black pepper

1 sixteen-ounce bag of mixed berries

bananas

french vanilla ice cream

Heat the chambord, red currant jelly and raspberry preserves in a saucepan over medium heat. Mix until simmering. Add the pepper and mix.

Place the berry mix in a blender. Add the chambord mixture and blend. Let it cool.

Slice bananas into lengths. Spoon ice cream into a bowl and surround with bananas. Spoon desired amount of dessert sauce over the ice cream and bananas.

baked pears

John E. Maling, Ph.D., Publisher, Mile High Press, Ltd.

Serves four. This is a simple and elegant finish to a meal.

4 pears, bosc, bartlett or your favorite, firm and unpeeled

1 tablespoon butter

4 tablespoons sugar

1 cup heavy cream

Spread half the butter over the bottom of a shallow baking dish large enough to hold the eight pear halves.

Sprinkle half the sugar over the buttered dish bottom. Place the pears in the dish, cut side down, spreading the rest of the butter over the skins of the pears. Sprinkle the remaining sugar over the top of the pears.

Bake for ten minutes.

Remove from the oven and pour the cream over the pears. Place them back into the oven and bake for another twenty minutes. Serve immediately.

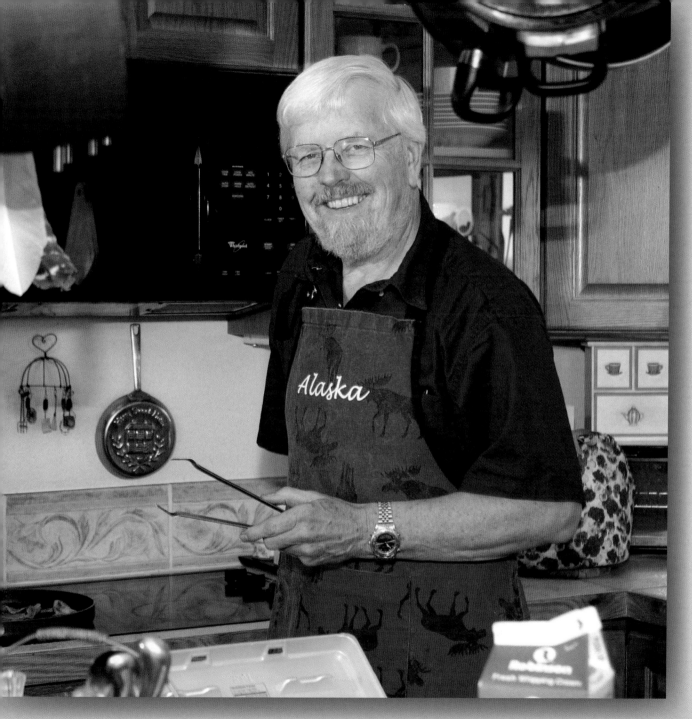

John Maling, Ph.D., President
Mile High Press, Ltd

Stepping into John Maling's kitchen, one is greeted with a friendly smile and warm hospitality as this "chef" stands behind the counter offering beverages to quench his guests' thirsty souls. Today, as president and owner of Mile High Press, he and author-wife Judith Briles, Ph.D., cook up books together. Judith is the author of twenty-three titles. Who are his other favorite authors? Mostly science fiction and action/thriller writers like Peter Hamilton and Robert Tannenbaum, he says.

Science, it seems, is never far from his thoughts. As a research physicist, John began his career at Stanford, spending ten years teaching others the art of exploration. From there he went on to Menlo College where he chaired the Science and Engineering Department.

John hasn't really gotten out of research. The pursuit of healthy home cooking still benefits from his scientific outlook. Says John, "Good nutrition avoids degenerative diseases and obesity."

ÿ John Maling, Ph.D. ÿ

ÿ **John McElrath** ÿ

tasty cheesecake

John A. McElrath, M.S.

John McElrath

Serves about six. For that low-fat touch, use low-fat cream cheese. John says, "I like to serve this topped with fruit." This is not your traditional cheesecake.

1-1/4 packages cream cheese, softened

juice of 2 oranges

2 caps lemon juice (1-1/2 teaspoons)

1-1/4 cups honey

1-1/2 packages knox gelatin

3 ounces warm water

1 graham cracker pie shell

Mix together the cream cheese and the fruit juices to a smooth consistency. Beat in the honey.

Dissolve the Knox gelatin in the water and add to the cream cheese mixture. Pour into the pie shell. Refrigerate the cheesecake for at least two hours.

Tip: You can make your own pie shell with two cups of crushed graham crackers mixed with two-to-four tablespoons melted butter. Then press it into a pie pan.

John McElrath has been a counselor for twenty-five years and is said to have a "no-nonsense approach reminiscent of Dr. Phil." He is a group facilitator and individual counselor on topics from communication to gender issues to relationships. John is also putting his many years of counseling experience into an upcoming book. He says that understanding the dynamics that flow between individuals unlocks truths to dealing effectively with conflicts.

In college, John had a reputation for producing delectable treats that would tantalize any college student with a bon appetite; that is, his buddies always knew where to go to get a good meal. John's enjoyment of cooking still serves him well. As a single father, he now prepares his culinary treats for appreciative son Christopher.

lobster wontons

Chef Mick Rosacci, Tony's Meats & Specialty Foods

This item can be prepared ahead and fried just before serving.

8 ounces cream cheese

1/8 teaspoon white pepper

1 clove finely grated garlic

1 teaspoon finely grated ginger

1 tablespoon lemon juice

2 tablespoons minced green onion

8-12 ounces cooked and shredded lobster meat

2 packages wonton wrappers

oil for deep frying

Combine cream cheese with the pepper, garlic, ginger and lemon, stirring well with a fork. Taste and adjust seasoning as desired. Gently fold in onions and lobster.

Brush the edges of six wontons with water. Place one-half teaspoon filling into each wonton, pressing out air, and sealing edges well to form a triangle. Stack on a plate, dusting each with cornstarch to avoid sticking. Store in refrigerator until time to fry.

Deep fry in hot oil until golden brown, serve immediately.

simple chili relleños

Jon Winterton, Ph.D., University of Colorado, Denver Center

Serves four. This is an easy way to make chili relleños without the mess of dipping them into batter before frying.

4 eggs, separated

3-4 teaspoons flour

2 cans whole chilies

1 pound sliced monterey cheese

oil for frying

salsa or green chili

Separate the eggs. Whip the egg whites until stiff. Fold yolks back into the egg whites. Add the flour.

Stuff each chili with Monterey cheese.

This is the easy part: heat the oil in a pan, not too much. Dab a spoonful of batter onto the hot oil. Add the chili, then spoon batter over the top of the chili. Turn over and fry the other side. Cook only a couple of minutes on each side. Serve with your favorite salsa or green chili.

lebanese baklava

Joe Sabah

Pistachios or your favorite nuts can be substituted for the chopped walnuts. Joe says, "This is a great recipe to invite friends for a Baklava-making party."

Baklava Topping

While the baklava is baking, combine the remaining three-fourths cup sugar, honey, one cup of water and orange rind in a saucepan. Then simmer baklava syrup for about twenty minutes, stirring occasionally, until it is syrupy. Remove the orange rind; cool and pour over baklava. This is best if the baklava is still warm or near room temperature and syrup is medium hot. Refrigerate until ready to use.

**When asked,
"How are you doing?"
Joe always responds,
"Counting my blessings."**

1 pound frozen phyllo sheets

1 cup melted butter

2 cups finely chopped walnuts

1/2 cup sugar

1/2 teaspoon ground cinnamon

3/4 cup sugar

3/4 cup honey

1 cup water

1 orange rind

Cut the phyllo pastry in half to fit your 13" x 9" x 1" pan. Work with one-half of the phyllo at a time. There is enough for two trays.

Keep pastry covered with a clean, damp cloth to prevent it from drying out. Brush a baking pan with melted butter. Place one pastry sheet in the pan and then brush it with melted butter. Continue adding and buttering until you have a stack of five sheets buttered.

Combine the nuts, sugar and cinnamon. Sprinkle three-to-five tablespoons nut mixture over the fifth buttered pastry. Repeat this process alternating five sheets of phyllo dough and three-to-five tablespoons nut mixture until you have a total of four layers.

Last, save the best sheet of phyllo for the top layer and cover with melted butter. Place the pan in your freezer for about twenty minutes. This allows the butter-phyllo combination to harden slightly.

With a very sharp knife, cut baklava pastry into two-inch diamonds. Then bake at 400 degrees until brown and crisp, about thirty or thirty-five minutes. Add Baklava topping (at left) and enjoy!

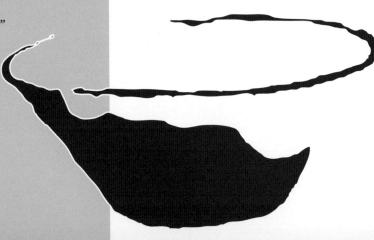

Joe Sabah, Author & President

Sabah & Company

Joe Sabah, nationally known author and speaker, is someone who encourages people to "sing the song they came to sing." A first meeting with Joe is an experience not easily forgotten. He usually starts by listening to your goals, pursuits and interests, asking pertinent questions, and then giving you the homework assignment toward expressing that song. To meet with this man is risky—you risk getting a boot in the right direction, stretching out into unmarked territory of personal pursuit. Enter only if willing to follow good advice.

Joe is the middle child of Lebanese parents; his mother became widowed when he was only nine. Life was not easy, but Joe certainly did not let that stop him. Joe has found that the secret to succeeding in life is finding that something you really like to do ... are willing to do it for nothing ... and then getting good enough at it that you actually GET PAID FOR IT.

Today Joe has mastered some great dishes, admitting it was done in self-defense. As a bachelor, he says, "I like to eat!" If you have tasted his baklava, you have Joe's Mom to thank. He grew up watching her prepare family meals.

ÿ *Joe Sabah* ÿ

chinese chicken wings

Mark A. Gagnon, Cognitive Solutions

Be sparing with the oyster sauce. A little goes a long way with this recipe.

1 large package chicken wings

1/3 cup oyster sauce

4 tablespoons soy sauce

1 tablespoon garlic powder

Heat oven to 400 degrees. Remove wings from the package and chop each into three pieces if using whole chicken wings, discarding the tip section. Place the other two sections on a greased cookie sheet.

Cook the wings for twenty minutes, turn them over and cook for twenty additional minutes. Then remove.

In a bowl combine the oyster sauce, soy sauce, and garlic powder. Stir well. Place the wings in the large bowl, coating the wings with the oyster sauce mixture.

Replace the wings on the cookie sheet and return to the oven for an additional twenty minutes. Drizzle an additional coating of sauce on the wings and serve immediately.

vanilla or chocolate custard ice cream

Chef Mick Rosacci, Tony's Meats & Specialty Foods

This serves a crowd, depending upon the quantity of each serving. It has a frozen custard flavor and is great if you are fond of the old-fashioned, hot-summer-day tradition of making ice cream.

12 egg yolks

1 to 1-1/4 cups white sugar or to taste

pinch salt

2-3 tablespoons vanilla or to taste

1 quart whipping cream

1 quart milk

In a large mixing bowl, beat egg yolks with sugar and salt until creamy. Whisk in remaining ingredients and place over a pot of simmering water, stirring regularly until the mixture coats the back of a spoon and tastes custardy.

Chill over a bowl of ice, stirring regularly, then lay a sheet of plastic wrap directly onto cream and chill thoroughly in refrigerator.

Pour into chilled ice cream maker and freeze according to manufacturer's directions. Store in freezer until time to serve.

Chocolate Variation: Reduce the sugar to approximately three-fourths cup and make according to directions, whisking six-to-ten ounces of Belgian milk chocolate into hot custard just before refrigerating.

Fruit Variation: Prepare recipe above. Chop about two cups fresh ripe fruit—stone fruits, berries and tropical fruits work the best; add a squeeze of lemon and just enough sugar to sweeten. Refrigerate for at least three hours. Stir into the ice cream right out of ice cream freezer; place in freezer if a firmer cream is desired.

Green Tea Variation: Whisk powdered Japanese green tea into hot custard to taste.

SURVIVORS!

hard sauce

Dave and Dori Samson

Dave remembers his parents serving this over bread pudding. You also could add this to Michael Sagrillo's Cinnamon Cranberry Bread Pudding and you'd have a sure hit. If doubling this recipe, do not double the bourbon, it will be too strong.

1 stick butter

1 cup sugar

1 egg beaten

1/4 cup bourbon

Add sugar to softened butter and beat well; add the egg and continue beating. Add the bourbon and mix well.

Cook the mixture in a double boiler on top of the stove until the sugar is dissolved and the mixture is creamy; do not let the mixture boil.

Serve this over filled crepes, pudding, or whatever; this hard sauce recipe is too terrific!

Ÿ Dave & Dory Samson Ÿ

This is a celebration and a special commemoration for two survivors. In 1999, Dory Samson was diagnosed with breast cancer. For the next year she, Dave and their two children together went through the rigors of this insidious disease. Then in February of 2003, Dory was diagnosed with cancer again. This time the cancer had spread to her spine and hip. For the next several months she and her family and friends again walked the bumpy road to recovery.

Not everyone who goes through this is as lucky as the Samsons. Some do not win the battle. In their wake are left, first and foremost, the husbands, then the children, extended family and friends. This disease knows no social barriers, no special privileges here. As with others, to watch this family walk through and do so victoriously is an honor; knowing them and being a part of their family of friends is a blessing.

So, to you who have gone through similar situations, this is a memorial, a testimony and celebration to the lives that are touched in a special way. Only those who walk hand-in-hand know the true trials of those of you who unwillingly have trudged down this path. To you who have gone through this kind of an ordeal, may our prayers and God's blessings go out to you.

cinnamon cranberry bread pudding

Michael Sagrillo, Chef and Owner, Bisetti's Ristorante

Michael says that day-old rolls work best for this recipe. However, any kind of rolls, even leftover doughnuts or sweet rolls, can be used effectively for this recipe.

1 pint heavy cream

1 pint whole milk

8 egg yolks

1/2 cup sugar

1 teaspoon vanilla extract

1 cup sun-dried cranberries

24 cinnamon rolls

Scold the milk and cream.

Whisk egg yolks, sugar and vanilla in a large bowl; mix the hot liquid into the egg mixture. Stir in the cranberries.

Tear the rolls into small pieces and add to the batter. Whisk batter to the consistency of cake batter leaving small, visible pieces of rolls. You may not need all of the rolls, so add them slowly.

Pour the batter into a greased baking dish and bake 350 degrees for thirty-five minutes until firm to the touch.

blueberry fried cheesecake

Ian Kleinman, Executive Chef, Indigo Restaurant

Serves several. This recipe can be prepared ahead, then frying and rolling in powdered sugar just before serving. This is a terrific do-ahead dessert for the holidays.

3 pounds cream cheese

3 cups sugar

10 egg yolks

1 teaspoon vanilla extract

2 cups frozen blueberries

1 cup powdered sugar

1 box phyllo dough

pam or butter spray

1 pint strawberries, fresh

1 pint blueberries, fresh

1/2 gallon canola oil

Place the cream cheese, one cup of the sugar, egg yolks and the vanilla extract in a mixer and mix until all ingredients are blended, making sure to scrape the bowl while mixing.

Place the cream cheese mixture in a baking dish and partially bake in a preheated 350-degree oven for twenty-five minutes. Remove and cool in the fridge.

Meanwhile, place the frozen blueberries and the remaining two cups of sugar in a saucepan. Cook on high heat until it is the consistency of syrup. Cool in the fridge.

When all of the ingredients are cool, place them in the mixer with the paddle attachment and mix. Place the mixture in a piping bag with a medium star tip. Take the phyllo out of the box. Be sure to place a damp towel over the dough when you are not working with it. The dough tends to dry out. Cut the phyllo in half. Take a single sheet and spray it with Pam, pipe a strip of the cheesecake filling onto the phyllo dough from one end to the other. Roll it up so it looks like a cigar. Wrap it in plastic and freeze.

Cook each for one minute in 350-degree oil, drain. Roll in powdered sugar, place on the plate and garnish with the fresh berries.

ÿ**Brad Freedberg**ÿ

brad's killer buffalo wings

Bradley S. Freedberg, Attorney at Law

Brad says, "The smaller the wings, the better." Serve with chunky blue cheese dressing with celery and carrot sticks.

1 large package whole chicken wings or small wings

2 tablespoons butter or margarine

2 cups durkee's or frank's red hot sauce

garlic powder to taste

black pepper to taste

chunky blue cheese dressing

celery sticks

carrot sticks

Brad learned family values through watching his own parents live out their beliefs.

If purchasing whole wing sections, cut the wing portions between drummette and wing, and between wing and wing tip. Discard wing tip. Rinse wings. Align in rows on broiler rack with a pan below to collect the fat, which will drip from the chicken. Or, align on a pre-heated outdoor grill. Sprinkle with generous amounts of garlic powder and black pepper.

Preheat oven to 425 degrees. Place wings in oven. Turn over wings after twenty minutes. (If using the outdoor grill, turn more frequently.)

Cook the wings an additional twenty minutes in the oven and turn again. You may need to turn them a third or even a fourth time. The key to this recipe is cooking these wings well so that all of the fat has cooked off without burning them. Meanwhile place a large pot on stove for the sauce.

On medium-high heat, melt two tablespoons butter or margarine. Once melted, add two cups Durkee's or Frank's red-hot sauce. Boil and reduce sauce until it thickens, about ten minutes. Once all wings are cooked to a crunchy golden brown on all sides, you are ready to mix with the sauce.

Remove from the heat, place the wings in the pot and mix to coat all wings with the sauce.

Bradley S. Freedberg,
Attorney at Law

"Stepping up to the plate" means something different to every individual. Bradley Freedberg defines it this way, "The time is right for me to respond to my vision and conviction and do my part to make my country the best it can be." As a father of two, husband, fellow countryman, and career politician, Brad believes in honesty, integrity and family values. As for politics, he says, "It is time to get rid of hypocrisy and deception in government. The time is now for me to move forward and act upon my convictions."

Brad began his culinary endeavors at the age of six when he prepared a surprise breakfast for his mom and dad. His desire to please others with his budding culinary delights grew as he continued to build his repertoire of dishes over the years. Since he didn't marry until he was thirty-five, Brad had a lot of time to practice stepping up to the plate.

Steve Knight, President

DNTLworks, Crown Seating, LLC,
Race Car Professional

This world-renowned race car driver and business turnaround specialist grew up in a West Virginia coal town. Dreaming of getting out, he left home early to follow his dreams, but he took Mom's recipes with him.

Steve credits his business success in large part to his employees. He includes them in all company decisions. "These (turnaround) companies are more then just me," he says, "My success depends on the people that work for me as much as it does on me. If they are unhappy, I won't be as successful." Crown Seating, LLC, is his eighth turnaround company.

As a race car driver over the past fifteen years, he has won 50 first-place finishes and driven most of the major courses in the United States, Canada, and Europe. He also won the American Le Mans Series LMP 675 Championship in 2002.

Thank heaven for Mom's recipes.

white chocolate mousse

Steve R. Knight, DNTL Works, Crown Seating, LLC, race car driver

Be careful adding sugar to the raspberry sauce—a little sweet will go a long way here; in fact the tartness of the raspberries will enhance this dessert.

12 ounces white chocolate, finely chopped

1 cup warm milk, divided

1 package unflavored gelatin

2 teaspoons vanilla

4 egg whites at room temperature

pinch salt

2 cups heavy cream

dash lemon juice

1 can frozen raspberries

Melt white chocolate in three-fourths of a cup of milk in the top of a double boiler over simmering water. Stir until smooth and remove from heat.

Soften gelatin in remaining one-quarter cup milk. Stir until dissolved, placing cup in hot water, if necessary. Add gelatin to chocolate; stir until very smooth. Stir in vanilla. Cool to room temperature.

Beat egg whites until foamy, add salt, and beat to almost stiff peaks. Mix a third of the whites into chocolate mixture. Gently fold in remaining whites in two batches.

Whip cream to soft mounds. Fold in the cream in three batches. Fold in lemon juice. Pour into serving bowl. Chill several hours.

For presentation, put frozen raspberries in blender and blend until liquid. Pour onto a small plate and put a scoop of mousse in the middle. Serve humbly, but enjoy.

ÿ Steve Knight ÿ

walnut potica

Randy Lee James, DC, Twin Peaks Chiropractic, P.C.

Pronounced "poteetza," this is a favorite Yugoslavian dessert. You can also find an Italian version, but this one is authentic Yugoslavian, handed down through the generations.

dough:

3 packages active dry yeast

1/4 cup lukewarm water

1 teaspoon flour & teaspoon sugar, for yeast

2 cups milk scalded

2 teaspoons salt

1/4 cup sugar

1 teaspoon butter

2 eggs, well beaten

7-1/2 cups flour, approximately

filling:

1-1/2 to 2 pounds ground walnuts

1 twelve-ounce can milk

6 well-beaten eggs

1 tablespoon butter

1 cup honey

1 cup sugar

Soften the yeast in warm water. Add a teaspoon of flour and sugar and let set about five minutes or until foamy.

Scald the milk and add butter, salt and sugar. Cool and add beaten eggs and yeast mixture. Add three-to-four cups of flour and beat with wooden spoon. Gradually add flour, keeping dough soft, not sticky.

Knead for fifteen minutes and place in a well-oiled bowl. Cover and let rise in a warm place until doubled in bulk. Do not punch down the dough after it has risen.

For the filling: Bring butter, milk, sugar and honey to a boil. Stirring continuously, add the walnuts. While stirring, slowly add beaten eggs; stir until eggs are partially cooked. Let cool to room temperature.

Spread a large cloth over a table and sprinkle liberally with flour. Roll dough out on the cloth to a one-eighth-inch thickness. Spread room temperature filling to edge of dough. Cut down the center. Using the cloth, roll each half like a jellyroll.

Place each onto greased baking pans and let rise one hour. Glaze rolls with one beaten egg white. Bake at 350 degrees for forty-five to sixty minutes or until golden brown.

lefsa

Eric Kloverstrom

This is a family recipe told to Candi Kloverstrom by her grandmother, Dagne Faust, and passed on to son Eric. Use the red potatoes for the best Lefsa. The secrets of Lefsa: after cooking, let it cool under a cloth, then put it into the freezer or eat it that day. Never put Lefsa into the refrigerator as refrigeration makes it hard and unedible..

10 good-sized potatoes

1 teaspoon salt

1 tablespoon sugar

1 small can condensed milk

3 tablespoons butter or margarine

1 cup white flour

Peel and cook the potatoes well. While hot, rice or mash the potatoes well and add one teaspoon salt, one tablespoon sugar, one small can condensed milk and three tablespoons butter or margarine. Mash well. Put the mixture through a ricer.

Spread in a large, flat pan and cook quickly. While cooling, do not let any of the water from condensation fall into the pan.

When very cold, add one cup flour and mix well and knead like bread dough for a couple of minutes.

Make small balls the size of an egg. Roll thin and bake on a griddle.

steve kelley's favorite palacsinta

Steve Kelley, 850 KOA, Colorado Morning News

This is a basic recipe for crepes. Steve's grandmother taught him how to make these Hungarian crepes when he was a child.

3 eggs

pinch of salt

1-1/4 cups flour

1 teaspoon sugar

1 cup milk

2 tablespoons canola oil

1 cup club soda

Mix eggs, flour, milk, sugar, salt, oil and club soda. Using a whisk to mix is the best way to ensure a smooth batter.

Heat an eight-inch frying pan. When the pan is hot, add a quarter spoon of oil. Pour a ladle of the batter into the pan, and gently tip and twist the pan so that the batter covers the entire bottom of the pan in a thin layer.

When the top of the batter bubbles, turn the crepes over and cook for seven-to-eight seconds longer. Remove the ready crepe and continue the process until the batter is gone.

Filling: Roll the crepes with your favorite jam, such as raspberry, strawberry, peach or apricot. Or sauté diced ham, beat with two eggs and prepare this as a thin omelet. Roll up in the crepes. For a vegetarian crepe, use sliced mushrooms, julienne carrots, and red and green peppers sautéed in olive oil.

In fact, Steve thought it was normal for business owners to feed their employees at the start of each day, as did his family.

Steve Kelley, Anchorman

850 KOA Colorado Morning News

Truth is, Steve does not cook. However, his grandmother once taught him how to make Palacsinta (crepes) when he was young. It took this book to get him cooking again! As Steve tells it, "There is a Hungarian chef at Clear Channel and he offered to show me how to prepare this dish my grandmother made years ago."

As one of seven children, Steve watched his grandmother and her sister prepare meals for family gatherings and also for the employees of their family-owned business. Gathering around the table was the norm, creating family tradition with culinary delights.

Steve's favorite story is about the time he was in the tenth grade and his English teacher, exasperated with his continual talking, sent him to the office. There, as a disciplinary action, he broadcast the school news to the whole school. Instead of putting an end to his antics, he discovered fellow students loved his discourse and this was the beginning of a career that has led him to 850 KOA as anchorman.

index of men

index of men

index of men

recipe index

recipe index